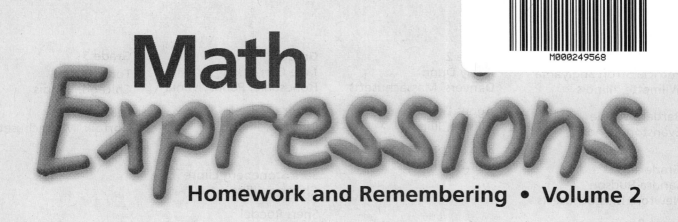

# Math Expressions

## Homework and Remembering • Volume 2

### Developed by
### The Children's Math Worlds Research Project

PROJECT DIRECTOR AND AUTHOR
## Dr. Karen C. Fuson

This material is based upon work supported by the
**National Science Foundation**
under Grant Numbers
ESI-9816320, REC-9806020, and RED-935373.

Any opinions, findings, and conclusions, or recommendations expressed in this material
are those of the author and do not necessarily reflect the views of the National Science Foundation.

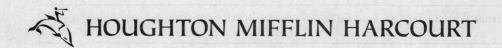

## HOUGHTON MIFFLIN HARCOURT

## Teacher Reviewers

**Kindergarten**
Patricia Stroh Sugiyama
Wilmette, Illinois

Barbara Wahle
Evanston, Illinois

**Grade 1**
Sandra Budson
Newton, Massachusetts

Janet Pecci
Chicago, Illinois

Megan Rees
Chicago, Illinois

**Grade 2**
Molly Dunn
Danvers, Massachusetts

Agnes Lesnick
Hillside, Illinois

Rita Soto
Chicago, Illinois

**Grade 3**
Jane Curran
Honesdale, Pennsylvania

Sandra Tucker
Chicago, Illinois

**Grade 4**
Sara Stoneberg Llibre
Chicago, Illinois

Sheri Roedel
Chicago, Illinois

**Grade 5**
Todd Atler
Chicago, Illinois

Leah Barry
Norfolk, Massachusetts

## Special Thanks

Special thanks to the many teachers, students, parents, principals, writers, researchers, and work-study students who participated in the Children's Math Worlds Research Project over the years.

## Credits

Cover art: (t) © Superstock/Alamy, (b) © Steve Bloom Images/Alamy
Illustrative art: Dave Klug
Technical art: Morgan-Cain & Associates

# Homework

**Solve.**

**1.** $5\overline{)28}$  $5\overline{)29}$  $5\overline{)30}$  $5\overline{)31}$  $5\overline{)32}$  $5\overline{)33}$

**2.** $5\overline{)36}$  $5\overline{)37}$  $5\overline{)38}$  $5\overline{)39}$  $5\overline{)40}$  $5\overline{)41}$

**3.** $5\overline{)201}$  $5\overline{)202}$  $5\overline{)203}$  $5\overline{)204}$  $5\overline{)205}$  $5\overline{)206}$

**4.** $5\overline{)154}$  $5\overline{)155}$  $5\overline{)156}$  $5\overline{)157}$  $5\overline{)158}$  $5\overline{)159}$

**5.** Describe any pattern you notice in the first row.

_____

_____

**Solve, using any method.**

**6.** $5\overline{)47}$    **7.** $5\overline{)14}$    **8.** $5\overline{)35}$    **9.** $5\overline{)49}$

**10.** $5\overline{)45}$    **11.** $5\overline{)200}$    **12.** $5\overline{)403}$    **13.** $5\overline{)104}$

**Solve.**

*Show your work.*

**14.** For the school field day, the students are divided into 5 same-size teams. Any extra students will serve as substitutes. If 243 students participate, how many students will be on each team? How many substitutes will there be?

_____

**15.** A fruit stand sells packages containing 1 peach, 1 pear, 1 apple, 1 banana, and 1 mango each. One week they sold a total of 395 pieces of fruit. How many packages did they sell?

_____

**16.** An orchard has 415 new cherry trees in 5 equal rows. How many trees are in each row? Are any trees left over?

_____

**Name** _____ **Date** _____

# Remembering

**Solve each problem as quickly as you can.**

1. 7 × 8 = _____  2. 6 × 4 = _____  3. 7 × 9 = _____

4. 6 × 6 = _____  5. 7 × 4 = _____  6. 8 × 9 = _____

7. 8 × 6 = _____  8. 7 × 5 = _____  9. 6 × 8 = _____

10. 8 × 4 = _____  11. 6 × 7 = _____  12. 8 × 5 = _____

13. 7 × 3 = _____  14. 8 × 8 = _____  15. 6 × 3 = _____

16. 7 × 6 = _____  17. 6 × 9 = _____  18. 8 × 3 = _____

19. 6 × 5 = _____  20. 8 × 7 = _____  21. 18 ÷ 6 = _____

22. 63 / 7 = _____  23. 6)‾54‾ = _____  24. 42 ÷ 7 = _____

25. 36 / 6 = _____  26. 6)‾48‾ = _____  27. 72 ÷ 8 = _____

28. 56 / 7 = _____  29. 6)‾30‾ = _____  30. 56 ÷ 8 = _____

**Tell whether each triangle is scalene, equilateral, or isosceles.**
**Then find its perimeter and area.**

31.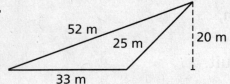

32.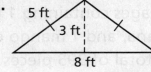

33.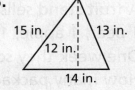

Name: _____   Name: _____   Name: _____

Perimeter: _____   Perimeter: _____   Perimeter: _____

Area: _____   Area: _____   Area: _____

Find the Unknown Factor

# Homework

**Solve.**

1. $5)\overline{150}$        $5)\overline{200}$        $5)\overline{250}$        $5)\overline{300}$        $5)\overline{350}$

2. $5)\overline{1,500}$        $5)\overline{2,000}$        $5)\overline{2,500}$        $5)\overline{3,000}$        $5)\overline{3,500}$

3. Describe how the repeating pattern in row 1 is different from the pattern in row 2.

_____

_____

4. Describe how the patterns are alike.

_____

_____

**Solve, using any method.**

5. $5)\overline{652}$                6. $5)\overline{6,502}$                7. $5)\overline{20,467}$

8. $5)\overline{837}$                9. $5)\overline{8,370}$                10. $5)\overline{16,894}$

**Solve.**

11. A park has a 5-foot wide straight path from one end of the park to the other. If the area of the path is 1,036 square feet, how long is it?

_____

_____

12. Joe counted 5 birch trees in the park. Sara counted 235 pine trees. How many times as many pine trees as birch trees did they count?

_____

_____

13. Joe saw 5 squirrels. Joe had 146 peanuts in his pockets. He fed all of them to the squirrels. If each squirrel got the same number of peanuts, how many did each squirrel get?

_____

_____

14. The main parking lot for the park has 5 identical rows of parking spaces. If there are a total of 615 spaces, how many cars can park in each row?

_____

_____

**Name** _____  **Date** _____

# Remembering

**Solve. Show your work on a separate sheet of paper.**

1. 73,169 + 42,508 = _____

2. 670,087 − 4,369 = _____

3. 302,136 − 9,747 = _____

4. 1,046,259 + 8,637 = _____

5. 273,450 − 18,094 = _____

6. 720,503 − 29,653 = _____

7. 11,947 + 202,638 = _____

8. 5,876,247 − 67,408 = _____

**Solve.**

9. Jerry's mother gave each member of the scout troop a box of apple juice. If there are 25 scouts in the troop and juice boxes come in packages of 5, how many packages did she need to buy?

_Show your work._

_____

10. Mazie has a goal of practicing her piano 3 hours a week. If she practices 25 minutes each day, does she reach her goal? Explain your thinking.

_____

_____

**Find the perimeter and area.**

11.

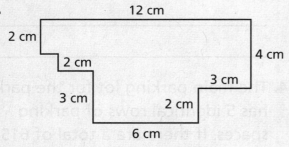

Perimeter: _____

Area: _____

12.

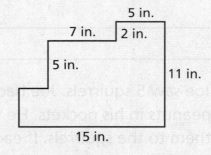

Perimeter: _____

Area: _____

Divide Thousands

**Name** _____ **Date** _____

# Homework

**Solve.**

1. 3)‾2‾1‾    3)‾2‾2‾    3)‾2‾3‾    3)‾2‾4‾    3)‾2‾5‾

2. 7)‾2‾1‾    7)‾2‾2‾    7)‾2‾3‾    7)‾2‾4‾    7)‾2‾5‾

3. Describe how the repeating pattern in row 1 is different from the pattern in row 2. Explain why.

_____

_____

**Solve, using any method.**

4. 9)‾2‾,‾3‾5‾9‾    5. 2)‾5‾,‾3‾8‾9‾    6. 4)‾1‾,‾6‾4‾8‾

7. 5)‾1‾,‾4‾5‾6‾    8. 8)‾2‾,‾5‾0‾6‾    9. 6)‾8‾,‾4‾7‾3‾

**Solve.**                                                     *Show your work.*

10. Mr. Beene brought 354 dishes to sell at the community yard sale. He sold sets of 3 dishes for $1.00 a set. If he sold all of his dishes, how much money did he make?

_____

11. Mr. James arranged his collection of 861 baseball cards in 7 equal rows. How many cards were in each row?

_____

# Remembering

This table shows the driving distances in kilometers between some cities of Mexico.

## Driving Distances in Mexico

|  | Cancún | Guadalajara | Mazatlán | Mexico City | Monterrey | Querétaro | Tapachula |
|---|---|---|---|---|---|---|---|
| **Acapulco** | 1,862 | 1,033 | 1,469 | 415 | 1,404 | 616 | 1,466 |
| **Ciudad Juárez** | 3,745 | 1,547 | 1,250 | 2,145 | 1,203 | 1,620 | 3,050 |
| **Mérida** | 319 | 2,231 | 2,752 | 1,555 | 2,213 | 1,765 | 1,382 |
| **Mexico City** | 1,874 | 676 | 1,197 | — | 989 | 210 | 1,220 |
| **Oaxaca** | 1,793 | 1,222 | 1,743 | 546 | 1,535 | 926 | 674 |
| **San Luis Potosí** | 2,287 | 348 | 869 | 413 | 537 | 203 | 1,633 |

**Use the table to answer problems 1–4.**

1. Between which two cities is the distance the shortest?

_____

2. Between which two cities is the distance the longest?

_____

3. What is the total driving distance of a trip from Ciudad Juárez to Mexico City and then from Mexico City to Tapachula?

_____

4. Which would be a greater distance?
   a. A round trip from Mazatlán to San Luis Potosí and back
   b. A one-way trip from Oaxaca to Mazatlán?

_____

# Homework

**Solve.**

1. 4)21̄    4)22̄    4)23̄    4)24̄    4)25̄

2. 6)21̄    6)22̄    6)23̄    6)24̄    6)25̄

3. Describe how the repeating pattern in row 1 is different from the pattern in row 2. Explain why.

_____

_____

**Solve, using any method.**

4. 8)6,758̄    5. 7)9,259̄    6. 3)1,774̄

7. 2)8,037̄    8. 9)3,385̄    9. 5)2,347̄

**Solve.**

10. There are 271 students registered for summer camp. If the camp has 8 cabins, how many campers live in each cabin?

_____

11. The camp has a rectangular batting cage where campers can practice hitting a baseball. It is 9 feet wide and has an area of 1,872 square feet. How long is the batting cage?

_____

12. The campers went to the beach. Sue collected 6 big shells in her bucket, and Josie collected 72 little shells. How many times as many shells did Josie collect as Sue?

_____

13. The camp playground is 55 feet wide by 72 feet long. It is divided into 6 play areas of equal size. What is the area of each play area?

_____

# Remembering

**Solve each problem as quickly as you can.**

1. 5)37

2. 5)24

3. 5)46

4. 5)31

5. 5)52

6. 5)26

7. 5)41

8. 5)39

9. 5)54

10. 5)21

11. 5)34

12. 5)43

**Solve.**

*Show your work.*

13. There are 30 students in Jamie's class. His mother bought apple muffins for the class. Apple muffins are sold in trays of 4, and Jamie's mother bought 8 trays. Did she buy enough apple muffins for each student in Jamie's class?

_____

14. In the school jump-rope contest, Lashaun jumped 37 times without missing. Then Maria jumped 4 times as many as Lashaun without missing. How many times did Maria jump without missing?

_____

**Write the name of each triangle according to its side lengths. Then find its perimeter and area.**

15.
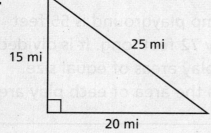

Name: _____

Perimeter: _____

Area: _____

16.
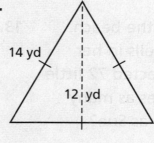

Name: _____

Perimeter: _____

Area: _____

17.
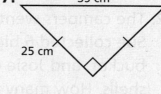

Name: _____

Perimeter: _____

Area: _____

Find Just-Under Quotient Digits

# Homework

**Solve by any method on a separate sheet of paper.**
**Then check your answer by rounding and estimating.**

**1.** $3\overline{)246}$          **2.** $6\overline{)75}$          **3.** $7\overline{)60}$

**4.** $4\overline{)58}$          **5.** $4\overline{)65}$          **6.** $8\overline{)91}$

**7.** $6\overline{)71}$          **8.** $6\overline{)86}$          **9.** $2\overline{)313}$

**10.** $3\overline{)256}$          **11.** $4\overline{)805}$          **12.** $5\overline{)927}$

**13.** $4\overline{)325}$          **14.** $4\overline{)378}$          **15.** $6\overline{)432}$

**16.** $6\overline{)490}$          **17.** $9\overline{)338}$          **18.** $8\overline{)658}$

**19.** $5\overline{)1,838}$          **20.** $4\overline{)2,715}$          **21.** $7\overline{)3,042}$

**22.** $3\overline{)6,127}$          **23.** $4\overline{)4,587}$          **24.** $4\overline{)9,029}$

**Solve.**

*Show your work.*

**25.** The area of Matt's bedroom is 96 square feet. If the room is 8 feet wide, how long is it?

_____

**26.** The fourth-grade students at Lincoln Elementary School are attending an assembly. There are 7 equal rows of seats in the assembly hall. If there are 392 fourth-grade students, how many students will sit in each row?

_____

**27.** Pablo is packing books into crates. He has 9 crates. Each crate will contain the same number of books. If he has 234 books, how many books can he put into each crate?

_____

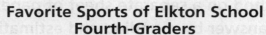

**Favorite Sports of Elkton School
Fourth-Graders**

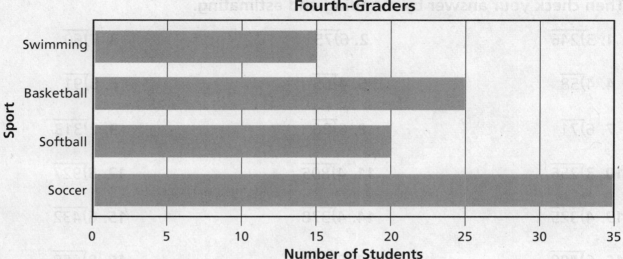

1. How many fourth-grade students said swimming was their favorite sport? _____

2. Which sport is most popular? _____ How many students chose it? _____

3. How many more students picked softball than swimming? _____

4. Altogether, how many students picked basketball or softball? _____

**Solve.**

**5.** 8 × 700 = _____        **6.** 7 × 931 = _____        **7.** 42 × 52 = _____

**8.** 300 × 4 = _____        **9.** 282 × 5 = _____        **10.** 81 × 73 = _____

Estimate to Check Quotients

# Homework

**Solve. Write the remainder as a whole number and as a fraction.**

1. 7)7,012                 2. 9)8,410                 3. 2)7,825

4. 5)3,512                 5. 6)6,618                 6. 8)7,225

**Solve.**

7. 8)$50.00                 8. 6)$49.62                 9. 9)$31.68

10. Write how each solution below is different and how it is the same.

a. 4)153  38 R1          b. 4)153  38 $\frac{1}{4}$          c. 4)$153.00  38.25

_____

_____

_____

_____

11. Write and solve two division problems in which the remainders mean different things.

_____

_____

_____

_____

_____

_____

# Remembering

**Solve by any method on a separate sheet of paper.**

1. $5\overline{)27}$     2. $8\overline{)99}$     3. $5\overline{)29}$     4. $6\overline{)95}$

5. $4\overline{)327}$     6. $9\overline{)314}$     7. $5\overline{)51}$     8. $8\overline{)93}$

9. $5\overline{)123}$     10. $4\overline{)173}$     11. $3\overline{)106}$     12. $4\overline{)66}$

13. Students worked in teams to rake leaves. The Red team filled 3 trash bags. The Green team filled 8 times as many bags. How many bags did the Green team fill?

_____

14. City workers trim the branches on the trees in 14 city parks. If there are 86 trees in each park, how many trees do the city workers trim?

_____

15. What is the side length in centimeters of a square that has an area of 9 square meters?

_____

16. What is the side length in meters of a square that has an area of 9 square meters?

_____

17. How many one-meter squares fit inside a square that has an area of 9 square meters?

_____

18. How many one-centimeter squares fit inside a square that has an area of 9 square meters?

_____

19. The garden store donated 8 packages of flowers to plant in a park. Five packages contain 12 flowers each. The rest of the packages contain 24 flowers each. How many flowers did the garden store donate in all?

_____

_____

**Name** _____    **Date** _____

# Homework

When the Johnson School fourth-grade classes were studying butterflies, they took a field trip to a butterfly garden.

**Use the correct operation or combination of operations to solve each problem.**

*Show your work.*

1. Nine buses of students, teachers, and parents went on the field trip. If 5 of the buses held 63 people each and the other buses held 54 people each, how many people went in all?

   _____

   _____

2. Some female butterflies lay their eggs in clusters. If one kind of butterfly lays 12 eggs at a time and another kind lays 18 eggs at a time, how many eggs would 8 of each kind of butterfly lay?

   _____

   _____

3. Teachers divided students into groups of 3. Each group of 3 wrote a report that had 9 pictures in it. The students used 585 pictures altogether. How many students were there in all?

   _____

4. Driving to and from the butterfly garden took 45 minutes each way. The students spent 3 hours in the garden and 30 minutes eating lunch. If the groups left the school at 9:00 A.M., what time did they get back?

   _____

   _____

   _____

**Name** _____ **Date** _____

# Remembering

**Solve.**

1. $4\overline{)34}$ 　　　 2. $9\overline{)80}$ 　　　 3. $6\overline{)39}$ 　　　 4. $8\overline{)27}$

5. $4\overline{)43}$ 　　　 6. $6\overline{)64}$ 　　　 7. $5\overline{)91}$ 　　　 8. $2\overline{)55}$

9. $5\overline{)72}$ 　　　 10. $3\overline{)49}$ 　　　 11. $4\overline{)93}$ 　　　 12. $9\overline{)111}$

13. $7\overline{)148}$ 　　　 14. $4\overline{)103}$ 　　　 15. $3\overline{)246}$ 　　　 16. $8\overline{)692}$

17. $3\overline{)346}$ 　　　 18. $7\overline{)906}$ 　　　 19. $5\overline{)529}$ 　　　 20. $4\overline{)805}$

21. $5\overline{)3,513}$ 　　 22. $4\overline{)3,281}$ 　　 23. $8\overline{)7,730}$ 　　 24. $7\overline{)2,884}$

**Solve.**

25. A farmer planted 120 tomato plants in 8 equal rows. How many plants are in each row?

_____

　　　　　　　　　　　　　　　Problem Solving

# Homework

**Solve. Write the remainder as a whole number and as a fraction.**

1. 4)9,813    2. 3)3,712    3. 5)7,082    4. 2)6,129

5. 7)8,063    6. 8)8,240    7. 3)4,319    8. 6)7,023

9. 5)8,115    10. 9)10,909    11. 7)9,315    12. 9)10,542

**Find the mean, median, and mode of each data set.**

13. 31, 42, 34, 21, 33, 31

    Mean: _____    Median: _____    Mode: _____

14. 561, 567, 561, 539

    Mean: _____    Median: _____    Mode: _____

15. 4, 3, 2, 7, 6, 4, 7, 4, 8

    Mean: _____    Median: _____    Mode: _____

**Solve.**

16. Hannah has four school workbooks. Their weights          *Show your work.*
    are 12 ounces, 14 ounces, 9 ounces, and 13 ounces.
    What is the mean weight of her workbooks?

    _____

17. Jose did 25 sit-ups on Monday, 20 on Tuesday,
    23 on Wednesday, 27 on Thursday, and 30 on Friday.
    What was the mean number of sit-ups he did?

    _____

18. Mrs. Kay works at a shoe store. Yesterday, she sold
    shoes in sizes 8, 6, 7, 9, 7, 8, and 5. What was the
    median shoe size she sold?

    _____

# Remembering

This table shows the cards that 6 members of the Sports Card club have in their collections.

| Club Member | Sport | | | |
|---|---|---|---|---|
| | Baseball | Basketball | Ice Hockey | Soccer |
| Alice | 10 | 7 | 6 | 12 |
| Kwami | 0 | 35 | 15 | 0 |
| Maureen | 3 | 21 | 0 | 36 |
| Nina | 12 | 10 | 1 | 2 |
| Ryan | 30 | 8 | 18 | 24 |
| Wally | 20 | 28 | 12 | 15 |

1. Which member has 3 more ice hockey cards than Wally?

_____

2. Write an additive comparison sentence to tell about the numbers of soccer cards that Alice and Wally have.

_____

3. Which member has 10 times as many baseball cards as Maureen? _____

4. Write a multiplication comparison sentence to tell about the numbers of basketball cards that Alice and Wally have.

_____

**Write the metric unit you would use to measure each of the following.**

5. Area of a field _____  6. Volume of a glass _____

7. Perimeter of a postcard _____  8. Distance between towns _____

# Homework

**Write each product or quotient. Look for a pattern.**

**1.** 7 × 10 = _____

    7 × 100 = _____

    7 × 1,000 = _____

**2.** 34 × 10 = _____

    34 × 100 = _____

    34 × 1,000 = _____

**3.** 80 × 10 = _____

    80 × 100 = _____

    80 × 1,000 = _____

**4.** 510 ÷ 10 = _____

    5,100 ÷ 100 = _____

    51,000 ÷ 1,000 = _____

**5.** 60 ÷ 10 = _____

    600 ÷ 100 = _____

    6,000 ÷ 1,000 = _____

**6.** 920 ÷ 10 = _____

    9,200 ÷ 100 = _____

    92,000 ÷ 1,000 = _____

**Multiply or divide.**

**7.** 84 ÷ 12 = _____

**8.** 132 ÷ 12 = _____

**9.** 12 × 7 = _____

**10.** 400 ÷ 100 = _____

**11.** 9 × 1,000 = _____

**12.** 3,000 ÷ 1,000 = _____

**13.** 66 ÷ 11 = _____

**14.** 8 × 12 = _____

**15.** 121 ÷ 11 = _____

**16.** 26,000 ÷ 100 = _____

**17.** 67 × 100 = _____

**18.** 9,900 ÷ 10 = _____

**19.** 108 ÷ 12 = _____

**20.** 10 × 11 = _____

**21.** 110 ÷ 11 = _____

**22.** 88 ÷ 11 = _____

**23.** 9 × 12 = _____

**24.** 60 ÷ 12 = _____

**25.** 12 × 12 = _____

**26.** 132 ÷ 11 = _____

**27.** 144 ÷ 12 = _____

**28.** 11,000 ÷ 1,000 = _____

**29.** 2 × 100 = _____

**30.** 3,000 ÷ 100 = _____

**31.** 99 ÷ 11 = _____

**32.** 96 ÷ 12 = _____

**33.** 11 × 11 = _____

**34.** 800 × 1,000 = _____

**35.** 430 ÷ 10 = _____

**36.** 16 × 1,000 = _____

**37.** 11 × 12 = _____

**38.** 120 ÷ 12 = _____

**39.** 55 ÷ 11 = _____

**40.** 400 × 100 = _____

**41.** 6,200 ÷ 100 = _____

**42.** 310 × 10 = _____

**43.** 12 × 10 = _____

**44.** 80 ÷ 10 = _____

**45.** 77 × 100 = _____

**Name** _____ **Date** _____

# Remembering

**Divide.**

**1.** 4)804      **2.** 3)225      **3.** 6)473      **4.** 5)5,525

**Write the place name of the underlined digit.**

**5.** 34,0<u>1</u>9 = _____      **6.** 2<u>7</u>3,505 = _____      **7.** <u>4</u>,617,800 = _____

**8.** What is the measure of ∠ABC? _____

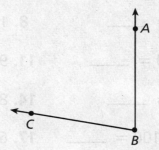

**Write an estimate to solve each problem.**

**9.** What is a reasonable estimate of the sum of 1,277 and 3,429?

_____

**10.** What is a reasonable estimate of the difference of 697 and 319?

_____

**Solve.**

**11.** Raphael has decided that the product of 19 and 51 is 969. Is Raphael's answer reasonable? Explain how an estimate can be used to help you decide.

_____

_____

Multiply and Divide by Powers of 10

# Homework

On a separate sheet of paper, draw an analog clock face to show the time.

**1.** 3:30 P.M.

**2.** 6:15 A.M.

**3.** 23 minutes past 3:30 P.M.

**4.** 43 minutes before 6:15 A.M.

**5.** 1 hour 18 minutes past 8:45 A.M.

**6.** 4 hours 28 minutes before 2:20 P.M.

**Find the number of hours and minutes that have passed between the times on each pair of digital clocks.**

**7.** AM 9:16 to AM 9:53

_____

**8.** PM 8:35 to AM 6:15

_____

**9.** PM 1:36 to PM 3:18

_____

**10.** AM 11:06 to PM 4:21

_____

The fourth-grade students at Fairview School are participating in Spring Games.

**11.** The Games start at 8:30 A.M., and the first break is at 10:15 A.M. How many minutes have passed when the first break starts?

_____

**12.** If Emma starts running at 10:45 A.M. and runs for 3 hours 20 minutes, at what time does she stop running?

_____

**13.** The afternoon mini-marathon will start at 1:15 P.M. The runners need 20 minutes to warm up. At what time do they need to start the warm-up period before the race?

_____

**14.** One game is a 20-person relay race. If each leg of the race takes about 4 minutes, about how many hours and minutes does it take to complete the race?

**15.** On a separate sheet of paper, write and solve a word problem about the passing of time.

# Remembering

**Divide.**

1. 675 ÷ 5 = _____  2. 471 ÷ 3 = _____  3. 875 ÷ 7 = _____

4. 987 ÷ 4 = _____  5. 362 ÷ 8 = _____  6. 446 ÷ 9 = _____

7. 575 ÷ 7 = _____  8. 216 ÷ 6 = _____  9. 870 ÷ 5 = _____

10. 1,025 ÷ 5 = _____ 11. 849 ÷ 3 = _____ 12. 2,106 ÷ 7 = _____

13. 667 ÷ 4 = _____ 14. 2,441 ÷ 8 = _____ 15. 969 ÷ 9 = _____

16. 972 ÷ 7 = _____ 17. 1,943 ÷ 6 = _____ 18. 1,011 ÷ 5 = _____

**Solve.**                                                    *Show your work.*

19. Two bottles of ketchup cost the same amount.
    One bottle contains 900 mL and the other contains
    1 L. Which bottle is the better buy? Explain.

    _____

    _____

    _____

20. One serving of milk is 250 mL. If you have
    4 servings each day, how many days will a
    2-L carton last? Explain.

    _____

    _____

    _____

21. A box is 25 cm long, 2 dm high, and 1 dm deep.
    What is the volume of the box in cubic
    centimeters? in cubic decimeters?

    _____

**Name** _____ **Date** _____

# Homework

## Simplify each expression.

**1.** $11m - 9m =$ _____   **2.** $y + 8y =$ _____   **3.** $13s - s =$ _____

**4.** $d + 2d + d =$ _____   **5.** $(9b - b) - 2b =$ _____   **6.** $104z + z =$ _____

**7.** $21 - (10 - 5) =$ _____   **8.** $(900 - 100) - 100 =$ _____   **9.** $90 - (50 - 1) =$ _____

**10.** $18 \div (27 \div 9) =$ _____   **11.** $(63 \div 7) \div 9 =$ _____   **12.** $40 \div (36 \div 9) =$ _____

**13.** $(48 \div 6) \bullet (11 - 9) =$ _____   **14.** $(3 + 17) \div (16 - 12) =$ _____

**15.** $(15 + 10) - (50 \div 10) =$ _____   **16.** $(19 + 11) \div (9 - 6) =$ _____

## Evaluate.

**17.** $c = 3$   **18.** $r = 2$   **19.** $w = 7$

$4 \bullet (7 - c)$   $(42 \div 7) \bullet (r + 1)$   $(72 \div 9) \bullet w$

_____   _____   _____

**20.** $m = 0$   **21.** $h = 14$   **22.** $p = 19$

$(12 \div 3) \bullet (5 - m)$   $45 \div (h - 5)$   $(p + 1) \div (9 - 4)$

_____   _____   _____

**23.** $v = 6$   **24.** $t = 1$   **25.** $g = 10$

$(18 - 9) + (2 + v)$   $(7 \bullet 2) \div t$   $(g + 90) \div (17 - 13)$

_____   _____   _____

## Solve for □ or n.

**26.** $7 \bullet (3 + 2) = 7 \bullet \square$   **27.** $(9 - 1) \bullet 4 = \square \bullet 4$   **28.** $8 \bullet (4 + 5) = \square \bullet 9$

$\square =$ _____   $\square =$ _____   $\square =$ _____

**29.** $6 \bullet (8 - 8) = n$   **30.** $(12 - 6) \div 3 = n$   **31.** $(21 \div 7) \bullet (5 + 5) = n$

$n =$ _____   $n =$ _____   $n =$ _____

# Remembering

**Divide.**

1. 5)515   2. 4)361   3. 8)740   4. 7)7,070

**Write the place value of the underlined digit.**

5. 5,6̲16 = _____   6. 13̲,044,652 = _____   7. 59̲1,756 = _____

**Write an estimate to solve each problem.**

8. What is a reasonable estimate of the product 9 × 99?

   _____

9. What is a reasonable estimate of the quotient 4,181 ÷ 6?

   _____

**Solve.**

10. Sarina has decided that the product of 59 and 100 is 59,000. Is Sarina's answer reasonable? Why or why not?

    _____

    _____

    _____

11. Which rotation is a 90° counter-clockwise rotation of the letter V?

    <   ∧   V   >
    A.   B.   C.   D.

Properties and Algebraic Notation

# Homework

1. A company is selling concert tickets by mail-order for $35 each. The shipping charge for any number of tickets is $10.

   Circle the letter of the expression below that represents the cost of purchasing 4 tickets.

   a. 4 + $35 • $10
   b. (4 • $10) + $35
   c. (4 • $35) + $10

2. The cost of Chantay's telephone plan is $7.50 per month plus $0.02 for every minute she uses her phone.

   In each expression below, $m$ represents the number of minutes Chantay uses her phone in a month. Circle the letter of the expression that represents her monthly cost.

   a. $7.50 + $0.02$m$
   b. $7.50 • $m$
   c. $7.50 + $m$ + $0.02

3. Write a real-world situation to represent the expression $c < $1$.

   _____

   _____

   _____

   _____

4. Write a real-world situation to represent the expression $n > 10$.

   _____

   _____

   _____

   _____

# Remembering

**Divide.**

1. $6\overline{)624}$        2. $5\overline{)417}$        3. $4\overline{)328}$        4. $8\overline{)8,168}$

**Write the place name of the underlined digit.**

5. 404,<u>7</u>34 _____     6. 3,<u>8</u>40,357 _____     7. 8<u>0</u>,274 _____

**Evaluate each expression.**

8. $d = 7$             9. $e = 48$           10. $f = 10$

$(16 - d) \div (1 + 8)$     $(e \div 8) \cdot 2$       $(f + 5) \div (6 - 1)$

_____             _____            _____

**Write an estimate to solve each problem.**

11. What is a reasonable estimate of the sum of 78 and 119?

_____

12. What is a reasonable estimate of the difference of 649 and 52?

_____

**Solve.**

13. Find the mean, median, mode, and range of the set of data shown below.

$$\{2, 2, 3, 9, 14\}$$

mean _____     median _____     mode _____     range _____

14. Which answers in exercise 13 can be found by using only mental math?

_____

_____

       Expressions and Inequalities

**Name** _____    **Date** _____

# Homework

**Substitute for the variable in each expression. Then simplify.**

**1.** $8 + m$ when $m = 5$ _____

**2.** $2k$ when $k = 7$ _____

**3.** $4r - 1$ when $r = 9$ _____

**4.** $10 \div (q + 3)$ when $q = 2$ _____

**Use mental math to solve each equation.**

**5.** $20 - d = 8$
$d =$ ____

**6.** $72 \div n = 9$
$n =$ ____

**7.** $7 + j = 16$
$j =$ ____

**8.** $3b + 1 = 25$
$b =$ ____

**9.** $4p - 5 = 3$
$p =$ ____

**10.** $10v + 2 = 42$
$v =$ ____

**11.** $6 \div (g + 2) = 1$
$g =$ ____

**12.** $8w - 4 = 60$
$w =$ ____

**13.** $(s \div 8) + 5 = 10$
$s =$ ____

**Circle the letter of the equation that best represents each situation.**

**14.** The cost of an item is $7.20, including tax. The amount of tax is $0.35. Which equation below can be used to find ($p$), the price of the item?

   **a.** $p \cdot \$0.35 = \$7.20$     **b.** $\$0.35 - p = \$7.20$     **c.** $p + \$0.35 = \$7.20$

**15.** Madison earns $9 for every hour she works. On Saturday she earned $54. Which equation below can be used to find the number of hours ($h$) Madison worked on Saturday?

   **a.** $h \cdot \$9 = \$54$     **b.** $\$54 \cdot h = \$9$     **c.** $\$9 \div h = \$54$

**16.** Quinn earns a monthly allowance of $20. He also earns $7 each time he mows the lawn. During the month of April, Quinn mowed the lawn four times. Which equation below can be used to find the number of dollars ($d$) Quinn earned during April?

   **a.** $4 \cdot (\$20 + \$7) = d$     **b.** $(4 \cdot \$7) + (4 \cdot \$20) = h$     **c.** $(4 \cdot \$7) + \$20 = d$

**Name** _____ **Date** _____

# Remembering

**Multiply or divide.**

1. $7\overline{)735}$

2. $6\overline{)572}$

3. $2\overline{)184}$

4. $9\overline{)9,915}$

5. $\begin{array}{r} 47 \\ \times\ 5 \\ \hline \end{array}$

6. $\begin{array}{r} 208 \\ \times\ \ 4 \\ \hline \end{array}$

7. $\begin{array}{r} 34 \\ \times 18 \\ \hline \end{array}$

8. $\begin{array}{r} 920 \\ \times\ \ 7 \\ \hline \end{array}$

**Write the place value of the underlined digit.**

9. 740,3<u>2</u>4 _____

10. 81,<u>4</u>20 _____

11. 6,<u>9</u>43,049 _____

**Solve for the variable in each equation.**

12. $5m = 55$

$m =$ _____

13. $18 + w = 18$

$w =$ _____

14. $n \div 3 = 9$

$n =$ _____

**Solve.**

15. The school day at Amanda's school begins at 8:30 A.M. and ends at 3:45 P.M. How long is Amanda's school day?

_____

16. The school day at Eduardo's school begins at 8:10 A.M. and is 6 hours and 55 minutes long. At what time does Eduardo's school day end?

_____

One-Step and Two-Step Equations

# Homework

## Connections

Describe a situation involving division and a remainder in which you would round up.

_____

_____

_____

_____

## Representation

Use pictures to show the mean of the set of numbers 7, 5, and 3.

## Communication

The Kite Club is divided into kite flying teams with 6 people on each team. There are 20 new people who want to join the club. Lupe says that not all of the teams will have an equal number of people. Is Lupe correct? Explain why or why not.

_____

_____

_____

_____

_____

## Reasoning and Proof

Otis measures a field and finds its length to be 100 units. Jason measures the same field, using a different unit of measure. He finds the length to be 300 units. State the relationship between the two units of measure used. Explain.

_____

_____

_____

_____

_____

**Name** _____  **Date** _____

# Remembering

**Solve.**

1. $9\overline{)37}$  2. $6\overline{)40}$  3. $5\overline{)23}$  4. $7\overline{)50}$

5. $5\overline{)56}$  6. $7\overline{)95}$  7. $2\overline{)63}$  8. $3\overline{)77}$

9. $4\overline{)86}$  10. $6\overline{)75}$  11. $8\overline{)94}$  12. $4\overline{)97}$

13. $5\overline{)107}$  14. $7\overline{)258}$  15. $4\overline{)389}$  16. $2\overline{)135}$

17. $5\overline{)641}$  18. $3\overline{)947}$  19. $6\overline{)816}$  20. $8\overline{)905}$

21. $6\overline{)3,716}$  22. $4\overline{)3,843}$  23. $7\overline{)5,479}$  24. $3\overline{)1,964}$

**Write the metric unit you would use to measure each of the following.**

25. perimeter of a field

_____

26. area of a state

_____

27. mass of a dog

_____

28. length of a pencil

_____

Use Mathematical Processes

# Homework

**Study each pattern. Then answer the questions that follow.**

1.

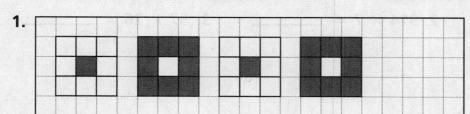

   **a.** Write a sequence of letters to represent the pattern.

   _____

   **b.** Draw the next term in the pattern.

2.

   **a.** Draw a shape to extend the pattern.

   **b.** Draw a **different** shape to extend the pattern.

3.

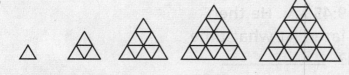

   **a.** Under each term in the pattern, write the number of small
      congruent triangles.

   **b.** How many triangles are in the sixth term of the pattern? _____

   **c.** Describe the pattern, using words.

   _____

   _____

   _____

   _____

4. Is the pattern in exercise 3 a repeating pattern or a growing pattern?
   Explain your choice.

   _____

   _____

# Remembering

**Multiply.**

**1.** 23 × 4 = _____    **2.** 914 × 7 = _____    **3.** 57 × 26 = _____

**Divide.**

**4.** 5)‾6‾9‾    **5.** 6)‾2‾7‾6‾    **6.** 4)‾2‾,‾1‾2‾8‾

**Solve.**

**7.** Basketball practice ended at 12:15 P.M. The basketball team practiced for 1 hour and 25 minutes. At what time did basketball practice start? _____

**8.** Juan records the temperature at 9:45 A.M. He then records the wind speed 12 hours later. At what time does Juan record the wind speed? _____

**9.** Karen buys 4 more CDs to put in her collection. Let *n* represent the number of CDs that Karen already had in her collection. Why does the expression *n* – 4 not represent the number of CDs that Karen now has in her collection?

_____

_____

**Use a protractor to measure each angle.**

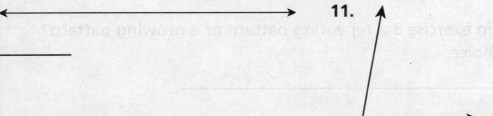

**10.** ⟵————————————⟶

_____

**11.**

_____

**Name** _____ **Date** _____

# Homework

The patterns below involve one operation. Describe each pattern, and identify the next term in it.

**1.** 2, 6, 18, 54, 162, 486, … _____

**2.** 975, 925, 875, 825, 775, 725, … _____

**3.** 4,000, 2,000, 1,000, 500, 250, … _____

**4.** 115, 145, 175, 205, 235, 265, … _____

**5.** 246, 211, 176, 141, 106, 71, … _____

The patterns below involve two operations. Describe each pattern, and identify the next two terms in it.

**6.** 1, 2, 4, 8, 10, 20, 22, … _____

**7.** 5, 10, 6, 11, 7, 12, 8, … _____

**8.** 3, 4, 8, 9, 18, 19, 38, … _____

**9.** 4, 2, 6, 4, 12, 10, 30, … _____

**Solve.**

**10.** A store owner gave each customer a number. He created a pattern to choose numbers, and gave a prize to the customers with these numbers. So far, he called numbers 1, 3, 9, 27, and 81. What are the next two numbers that will be called? Explain how you found your answer.

_____

_____

_____

**Name** _____ **Date** _____

# Remembering

**Multiply.**

1. 48 × 6 = _____   2. 496 × 5 = _____   3. 54 × 11 = _____

**Divide.**

4. 88 ÷ 9 = _____   5. 917 ÷ 7 = _____   6. 4,187 ÷ 8 = _____

**Find a reasonable estimate for each problem.**

7. 38 × 24 _____   8. 524 ÷ 6 _____

**Evaluate.**

9. $a = 8$   10. $c = 5$   11. $w = 10$

$(7 + a) - 3$ _____   $(8 ÷ 4) • (c - 2)$ _____   $(36 ÷ 4) • w$ _____

**Solve.**

12. Ken buys 3 packages of tomato seeds. Each package has 16 seeds. He plants an equal amount of seeds in 4 rows of his garden. How many tomato seeds does Ken plant in each row of his garden? _____

13. Which two figures look congruent? Explain how you know.

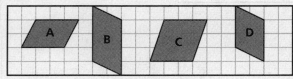

_____

_____

Numerical Patterns

**Name** _____   **Date** _____

# Homework

Use the operation or operations to complete the table.

**1.**

| Add 9 | | | | | |
|---|---|---|---|---|---|
| **Input** | | 2 | | | 12 |
| **Output** | 12 | | 18 | 14 | |

**2.**

| Subtract 6, then multiply by 2 | | | | | |
|---|---|---|---|---|---|
| **Input** | 10 | 8 | 11 | 7 | 9 |
| **Output** | | | | | |

Use the table to complete exercises 3 and 4.

| Number of Boxes (*b*) | 1 | 2 | 3 | 4 | 5 | 6 | 7 | 8 |
|---|---|---|---|---|---|---|---|---|
| Number of Crayons (*c*) | 6 | 12 | 18 | 24 | 30 | 36 | 42 | 48 |

**3.** Using words, write the rule of the function.

_____

**4.** Using the variables *b* and *c*, write an equation
which shows that the number of crayons (*c*) is a function
of the number of boxes (*b*).

_____

**Solve.**

**5.** Below the table, write an equation that uses
the variables *x* and *y* and shows *y* as a function of *x*.

| *x* | 4 | 5 | 6 | 7 | 8 |
|---|---|---|---|---|---|
| *y* | 1 | 2 | 3 | 4 | 5 |

_____

**6.** Each student brought in 9 cans to recycle. Write
an equation to represent the total number of cans
(*c*) for any number of students (*s*).

_____

**Name** _____  **Date** _____

# Remembering

**Multiply.**

| 1. 71 | 2. 403 | 3. 58 |
|---|---|---|
| × 5 | × 7 | × 31 |

**Divide.**

4. 6)̄92

5. 3)̄422

6. 9)̄9,828

**Find the mean, median, mode, and range of each data set.**

7. 3, 6, 2, 3, 8, 2

Mean: _____    Median: _____

Mode: _____    Range: _____

8. 10, 15, 10, 13, 11, 15, 10

Mean: _____    Median: _____

Mode: _____    Range: _____

**Solve for the variable in each equation.**

9. $n + 5 = 36$

   $n =$ _____

10. $m \div 8 = 30$

    $m =$ _____

11. $6w = 30$

    $w =$ _____

**Decide if the pair of figures appears to be similar.**
**Write *yes* or *no*. Explain how you know.**

12.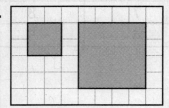

_____

_____

13.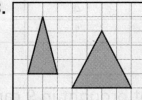

_____

_____

Functions

# Homework

Use the coordinate plane below to answer
the questions that follow.

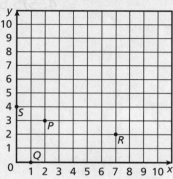

**Write an ordered pair to represent the location
of each point.**

**1.** point *P* _____ **2.** point *Q* _____ **3.** point *R* _____ **4.** point *S* _____

**Plot and label a point at each location.**

**5.** point *W* at (3, 9) **6.** point *X* at (3, 5) **7.** point *Y* at (9, 5)

**Solve.**

**8.** Suppose points *W*, *X*, and *Y*, represent three vertices
of rectangle *WXYZ*. Where should point *Z* be plotted
to form the rectangle?

_____

Plot and label point *Z*. Then use a ruler to draw
the rectangle.

**9.** What ordered pair represents the point at the center
of the rectangle?

_____

**10.** Explain how subtraction can be used to find the lengths
of line segment *WX* and line segment *XY*.

_____

_____

# Remembering

**Divide.**

1. $4\overline{)820}$
2. $8\overline{)250}$
3. $2\overline{)125}$
4. $5\overline{)5,615}$

**Simplify each expression.**

5. $(54 \div 9) \cdot (12 - 4) =$ _____
6. $(8 + 7) \div (15 - 10) =$ _____
7. $(6 + 5) - (70 \div 7) =$ _____
8. $(23 - 17) + (3 \cdot 2) =$ _____

9. Write the prime factorization of 45. _____

10. Explain why 45 is a multiple of each factor you wrote for exercise 9.

_____

11. Is 29 a prime number? Explain why or why not.

_____

**Write an estimate to solve each problem.**

12. What is a reasonable estimate of the sum 18,759 + 31,044?

_____

13. What is a reasonable estimate of the difference 6,052 − 978?

_____

**Solve.**

14. DeJuan has decided that the product of 43 and 1,000 is 4,300. Is DeJuan's answer reasonable? Why or why not?

_____

_____

# Homework

1. Complete the function table.

2. Write the rule of the function table, using words.

   _____

3. Using the variables *x* and *y*, write an equation that shows that *y* is a function of *x*.

   _____

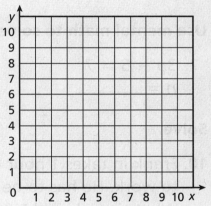

| x | y |
|---|---|
| 0 | 0 |
| 1 | 2 |
| 2 | 4 |
| 3 |   |
|   | 8 |
| 5 |   |

4. Each ordered pair in the table represents a point. Use the table to write each set of ordered pairs.

   _____

5. On the coordinate plane at the right, use the ordered pairs to plot and label each point. Then use a ruler and draw a segment to connect the points.

6. Compare the *y*-coordinate of each point to its *x*-coordinate. Describe the relationship, using words.

   _____

7. How does the pattern on the coordinate plane compare to the pattern in the function table?

   _____

8. What is the *y*-coordinate of a point on the line graph if the *x*-coordinate is 8? Explain how you found your answer.

   _____

**Name** _____  **Date** _____

# Remembering

**Multiply.**

**1.** $36 \times 5 =$ _____

**2.** $245 \times 3 =$ _____

**3.** $24 \times 23 =$ _____

**Divide.**

**4.** $4\overline{)97}$

**5.** $3\overline{)749}$

**6.** $7\overline{)8,467}$

**Use mental math to solve for the variable in each equation.**

**7.** $3n - 5 = 7$

$n =$ _____

**8.** $4m + 8 = 16$

$m =$ _____

**9.** $(a \div 3) - 4 = 6$

$a =$ _____

**Solve.**

**10.** Franklin takes 1 hour 45 minutes to get to work. He has to be at work at 6:30 P.M. What time should Franklin leave to get to work? _____

**11.** There are 85 students sitting in the bleachers. Each row of the bleachers seats 7 students. How many rows of the bleachers will the students be sitting in? _____

**12.** Estimate the area of the pond in square units. Explain how you found your estimate.

_____

_____

_____

_____

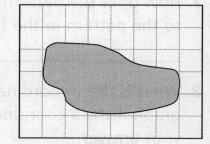

Graph a Function

# Homework

This table shows continuous data. Use the table for exercises 1–3.

1. Is the trend of data increasing or decreasing? Explain your answer.

   _____

   _____

   _____

| Morning Temperatures | |
|---|---|
| Time | Temperature (°F) |
| 12 A.M. | 44 |
| 2 A.M. | 43 |
| 4 A.M. | 40 |
| 6 A.M. | 38 |
| 8 A.M. | 38 |

2. Could you use the given data to predict the temperature at 5 A.M.? Explain your answer.

   _____

   _____

3. If you create a line graph from the data, what will the line look like between 4 A.M. and 6 A.M.?

   _____

**Use the graph for exercises 4 and 5.**

4. List the distance traveled at each hour.

   _____

   _____

5. Explain what could have happened between hours 4 and 5. Support your answer.

   _____

   _____

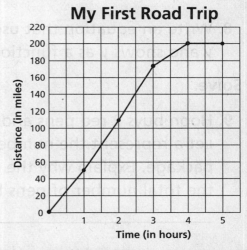

**My First Road Trip**

6. On a separate sheet of grid paper, make a line graph that displays the data in the table.

| My Second Road Trip | |
|---|---|
| Time (hours) | Distance (miles) |
| 0 | 0 |
| 1 | 60 |
| 2 | 130 |
| 3 | 190 |
| 4 | 200 |

# Remembering

**Multiply.**

**1.** $64 \times 9 =$ _____

**2.** $387 \times 6 =$ _____

**3.** $74 \times 58 =$ _____

**Divide.**

**4.** $54 \div 7 =$ _____

**5.** $389 \div 4 =$ _____

**6.** $3,284 \div 4 =$ _____

**Use the function table for exercises 7 and 8.**

| $x$ | 3 | 4 | 5 | 6 | 7 | 8 | |
|-----|---|---|---|---|---|---|---|
| $y$ | 12 | 16 | 20 | 24 | 28 | | 40 |

**7.** Complete the function table.

**8.** Write an equation that uses the variables $x$ and $y$ and shows $y$ as a function of $x$. _____

**Solve.**

**9.** Hoon buys 2 red pens and 3 packages of blue pens. Let $a$ represent the number of blue pens in each package. Explain why the equation $3a + 2$ represents the total number of pens Hoon bought.

_____

_____

**10.** Look at Figure A. Circle the shaded figure below that shows how Figure A looks after it is rotated 270° clockwise.

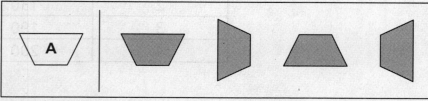

Read a Line Graph

# Homework

**Write the chain of unit fractions for each fraction.**

1. $\frac{2}{4}$ = _____

2. $\frac{5}{8}$ = _____

3. $\frac{2}{6}$ = _____

4. $\frac{7}{8}$ = _____

5. $\frac{4}{12}$ = _____

6. $\frac{6}{12}$ = _____

7. $\frac{8}{12}$ = _____

8. $\frac{4}{6}$ = _____

**Name the fraction for each chain of unit fractions.**

9. $\frac{1}{4} + \frac{1}{4} + \frac{1}{4}$ = _____

10. $\frac{1}{8} + \frac{1}{8} + \frac{1}{8}$ = _____

11. $\frac{1}{8} + \frac{1}{8} + \frac{1}{8} + \frac{1}{8}$ = _____

12. $\frac{1}{12} + \frac{1}{12} + \frac{1}{12} + \frac{1}{12} + \frac{1}{12} + \frac{1}{12} + \frac{1}{12}$ = _____

13. $\frac{1}{12} + \frac{1}{12}$ = _____

14. $\frac{1}{6} + \frac{1}{6} + \frac{1}{6}$ = _____

15. $\frac{1}{6} + \frac{1}{6} + \frac{1}{6} + \frac{1}{6} + \frac{1}{6}$ = _____

16. $\frac{1}{8} + \frac{1}{8} + \frac{1}{8} + \frac{1}{8} + \frac{1}{8} + \frac{1}{8}$ = _____

**Write three things you learned today about fractions.**

_____

_____

_____

_____

**Name** _____   **Date** _____

# Remembering

**Solve.**

1. 942 + 4,605 = _____

2. 31,582 − 9,406 = _____

3. 72 × 54 = _____

4. 847 ÷ 3 = _____

5. 178 + 45,947 = _____

6. 56,168 − 963 = _____

7. 93 × 27 = _____

8. 1,983 ÷ 5 = _____

9. 23,019 + 1,932 = _____

10. 52,635 − 7,068 = _____

11. 68 × 36 = _____

12. 4,294 ÷ 7 = _____

**Find the perimeter and area for each group of shapes. Show your work.**

13.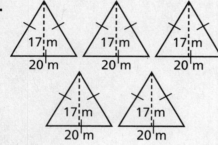

Perimeter: _____

Area: _____

14.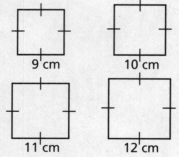

Perimeter: _____

Area: _____

15.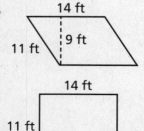

Perimeter: _____

Area: _____

Understand Fractions

# Homework

**Name the fraction of the shape that is shaded and the fraction of the shape that is not shaded. Then, write an equation that shows how the two fractions make one whole.**

1.

shaded: _____

unshaded: _____

equation: _____

2.

shaded: _____

unshaded: _____

equation: _____

3.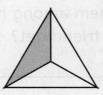

shaded: _____

unshaded: _____

equation: _____

4.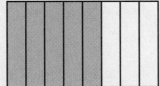

shaded: _____

unshaded: _____

equation: _____

5.

shaded: _____

unshaded: _____

equation: _____

**Name the fraction that will complete each equation.**

6. $1 = \frac{3}{3} = \frac{1}{3} +$ _____

7. $1 = \frac{8}{8} = \frac{3}{8} +$ _____

8. $1 = \frac{4}{4} = \frac{2}{4} +$ _____

9. $1 = \frac{10}{10} = \frac{7}{10} +$ _____

10. $1 = \frac{6}{6} = \frac{5}{6} +$ _____

11. $1 = \frac{9}{9} = \frac{8}{9} +$ _____

12. $1 = \frac{7}{7} = \frac{4}{7} +$ _____

13. $1 = \frac{12}{12} = \frac{9}{12} +$ _____

**Solve.**                                    *Show your work.*

14. By Friday afternoon $\frac{3}{12}$ of the biographies in the school library had been checked out. What fraction of the biographies were still in the library?

_____

# Remembering

**Solve.**

*Show your work.*

1. Martin has 13 red marbles, 25 silver marbles, and 74 green marbles. If he mixes them all together and divides them among his 8 friends, how many marbles will each friend get?

   _____

2. Julio bought a bag of 70 oranges. His family ate 7 of the oranges. Julio divided the rest into 7 bags. How many oranges were in each bag?

   _____

3. Ricky has a box of 24 crayons. Jane's box has 8 times as many crayons as Ricky's. How many crayons do Ricky and Jane have altogether?

   _____

**Find perimeter and area of each figure.
(Note: All angles are right angles.)**

4.
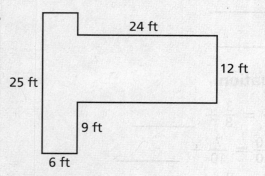

Perimeter: _____

Area: _____

5.
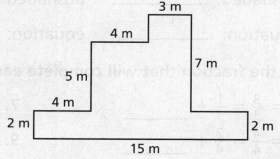

Perimeter: _____

Area: _____

**Simplify each expression.**

6. $12a - (6a + a) =$ _____

7. $n + 6n + 2n =$ _____

8. $128y - 25y =$ _____

Fraction Partners of One Whole

# Homework

**Write < or > to make each statement true.**

1. $\frac{1}{5}$ ◯ $\frac{1}{4}$

2. $\frac{6}{12}$ ◯ $\frac{5}{12}$

3. $\frac{4}{10}$ ◯ $\frac{4}{11}$

4. $\frac{3}{5}$ ◯ $\frac{4}{5}$

5. $\frac{3}{7}$ ◯ $\frac{3}{8}$

6. $\frac{7}{9}$ ◯ $\frac{8}{9}$

**Solve. Explain your answers.**

*Show your work.*

7. Juan took $\frac{2}{12}$ of the fruit salad and Harry took $\frac{3}{12}$ of the same salad. Who took more of the salad?

_____

_____

_____

8. Kim drank $\frac{1}{3}$ of a carton of milk. Joan drank $\frac{1}{4}$ of a carton. Who drank more?

_____

_____

9. Maria read $\frac{1}{8}$ of a story. Darren read $\frac{1}{7}$ of the same story. Who read more of the story?

_____

_____

_____

10. Write 2 things you learned today about comparing fractions.

_____

_____

_____

11. Write and solve a fraction word problem of your own.

_____

_____

_____

**Name** _____  **Date** _____

# Remembering

**Solve.**  *Show your work.*

1. Mattie's summer reading goal was 3,000 pages. She has already read 147 pages. How many more pages must she read to reach her goal?

   _____

2. Jin-Lee read that about 9 inches of snow has the same amount of water as 1 inch of rain. At Jin-Lee's house it rained 2 inches one day and 3 inches the next day. If it had snowed instead, how many inches of snow would have fallen at Jin-Lee's house over the 2 days?

   _____

3. Austin's family drove 1,215 miles from New York to Florida. They drove for 3 days and traveled the same distance each day. How many miles did they travel each day?

   _____

**Find the perimeter and area of each figure. (Note: All angles are right angles.)**

4.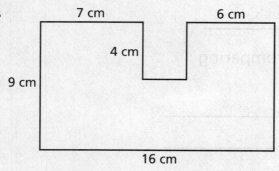

   Perimeter: _____

   Area: _____

5.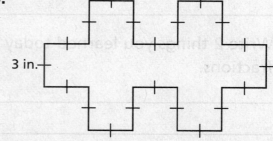

   Perimeter: _____

   Area: _____

**Simplify each expression.**

6. $(118 + 18) \div (12 - 8) =$ _____

7. $(40 \div 2) \cdot (16 + 11) =$ _____

Compare Fractions

# Homework

1. Draw a small, a medium, and a large square. Shade $\frac{1}{6}$ of each.

2. Draw a small, a medium, and a large circle. Shade $\frac{3}{4}$ of each.

3. Draw a short, a medium, and a long rectangle. Shade $\frac{3}{5}$ of each.

4. Look at the different size shapes you shaded in problems 1–3. Describe what they show about fractions of different wholes.

   _____

   _____

   _____

**Solve.**                                              *Show your work.*

5. Kris ate $\frac{3}{8}$ of a pizza and Kim ate $\frac{4}{8}$ of the same pizza. Did they eat the whole pizza? Explain.

   _____

6. Amena ate $\frac{1}{2}$ of a sandwich. Lavonne ate $\frac{1}{2}$ of a different sandwich. Amena said they ate the same amount. Lavonne said Amena ate more. Could Lavonne be correct? Explain your thinking.

   _____

   _____

   _____

# Remembering

**Draw, divide, and color or shade a shape of your choice to show each fraction. Be sure to divide the shape into equal-size parts. Label the whole and all the parts.**

1. $\frac{3}{8}$

2. $\frac{3}{4}$

3. $\frac{8}{10}$

4. $\frac{1}{5}$

5. $\frac{7}{12}$

6. $\frac{6}{7}$

7. $\frac{2}{6}$

8. $\frac{3}{9}$

**Solve.**

9. $72 \times 3 =$

10. $68 \times 5 =$

11. $109 \times 7 =$

12. $413 \times 9 =$

_____

_____

_____

_____

13. $3\overline{)74}$

14. $6\overline{)54}$

15. $7\overline{)609}$

16. $9\overline{)640}$

17. $7\overline{)84}$

18. $8\overline{)95}$

19. $3\overline{)643}$

20. $8\overline{)471}$

**Tell which metric unit you would use for each measurement.**

21. the length of a paper clip _____

22. the area of a field _____

23. the length of a driveway _____

24. the area of a postcard _____

25. the distance between cities _____

Fractions of Different Size Wholes

1. Use a compass or a piece of paper to draw two different-sized circles. Label the parts of both circles: center, radius, diameter, and circumference. Then measure the diameter of each circle in centimeters.

2. Explain how to calculate the circumference of your circles.

   _____

   _____

**Estimate the circumference of each circle. Use $\pi = 3$ to make your estimates.**

3.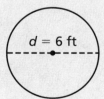
   $d = 6$ ft

   _____

4.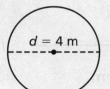
   $d = 4$ m

   _____

5.
   $d = 8$ yd

   _____

6.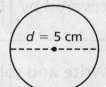
   $d = 5$ cm

   _____

**Name** _____ **Date** _____

# Remembering

**Add or subtract.**

**1.** 4,679 + 135,820

_____

**2.** 63,159,240 − 42,851

_____

**3.** 35,947,821 − 6,538,041

_____

**4.** 594,163 + 42,750

_____

**5.** 729,315 − 40,856

_____

**6.** 903,492,517 − 65,340

_____

**7.** 87,624 + 61,305,087

_____

**8.** 24,678,305 − 94,513

_____

**9.** 1,649,315 − 276,894

_____

**Solve.**                                                    *Show your work.*

**10.** A football field is 1,000 yd long. Each of the two end zones adds an extra 10 yd. The field is 160 ft wide. What is the area of the whole field?

_____

**11.** An apartment building has 45 windows on each side. Each window is a rectangle that is 2 ft × 4 ft. What is the area of glass in the building?

_____

**12.** A rectangle has an area of 8 sq in. and a square has an area of 9 sq in. What is the area of a surface covered by 16 squares and 14 rectangles?

_____

**13.** Write and solve a multi-step word problem about measurement.

_____

_____

_____

Circles

# Homework

Luisa is in fourth grade. Her brother Emilio is in high school. These circle graphs show how they spend their days.

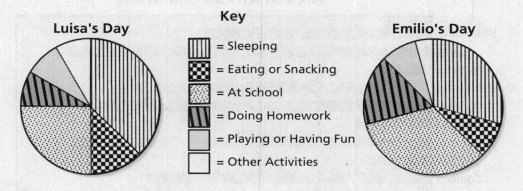

**Key**

Luisa's Day

Emilio's Day

= Sleeping
= Eating or Snacking
= At School
= Doing Homework
= Playing or Having Fun
= Other Activities

**1.** Who usually spends more hours eating or snacking?

_____

**2.** Which two activities usually occupy half of Luisa's day?

_____

**3.** On what activity do Luisa and Emilio usually spend about the same amount of time?

_____

**4.** Luisa spends about 2 hours doing homework. About how much time does Emilio spend doing homework?

_____

**Solve.**

**5.** The part of Emilio's graph that shows "Other Activities" represents 1 hour. Based on the size of this part, estimate the number of whole hours Emilio spends on Playing or Having Fun.

_____

**6.** On a separate sheet of paper, make a circle graph to show how you spend your time on a typical school day. Then write two questions to compare your day with Luisa's or Emilio's day.

**Name** _____ **Date** _____

# Remembering

This bar graph shows the area of some countries in Africa.

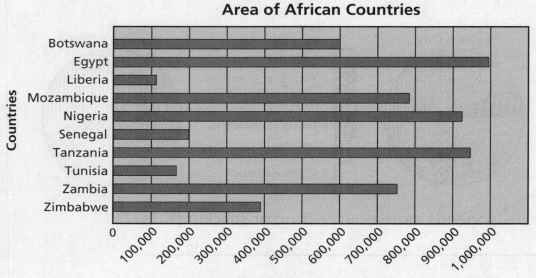

**Area of African Countries**

Countries (top to bottom): Botswana, Egypt, Liberia, Mozambique, Nigeria, Senegal, Tanzania, Tunisia, Zambia, Zimbabwe

Area in Square Kilometers (0; 100,000; 200,000; 300,000; 400,000; 500,000; 600,000; 700,000; 800,000; 900,000; 1,000,000)

1. Which two countries are the smallest in area?

_____

2. Which three countries are more than 900,000 square kilometers in area?

_____

3. What is the area of Zambia? How do you know?

_____

_____

4. Which country is about three times the area of Senegal?

_____

5. What is the combined approximate area of Zimbabwe and Mozambique? Show your work.

_____

6. On a separate sheet of paper, write and solve two word problems about the bar graph.

Explore Circle Graphs

**Name** _____ **Date** _____

# Homework

**Solve.**

1. $\frac{4}{8} + \frac{2}{8} =$ _____

2. $\frac{3}{11} + \frac{6}{11} =$ _____

3. $\frac{3}{4} - \frac{2}{4} =$ _____

4. $\frac{3}{5} + \frac{4}{5} =$ _____

5. $\frac{2}{6} + \frac{1}{6} =$ _____

6. $\frac{6}{7} - \frac{2}{7} =$ _____

7. $\frac{5}{12} + \frac{4}{12} =$ _____

8. $\frac{9}{10} - \frac{3}{10} =$ _____

9. $\frac{8}{9} - \frac{4}{9} =$ _____

**Solve.**

*Show your work.*

10. Sue is driving to see her mom. The first day she traveled $\frac{2}{5}$ of the distance. The next day she traveled another $\frac{2}{5}$ of the distance. What fraction of the distance has she driven?

_____

11. When Keshawn sharpens her pencil, she loses about $\frac{1}{12}$ of the length. One day, she sharpened her pencil 3 times. The next day she sharpened the same pencil 5 times. What fraction of the pencil did Keshawn sharpen away?

_____

12. One day, a flower shop sold $\frac{7}{10}$ of its roses in the morning and $\frac{2}{10}$ of its roses in the afternoon. What fraction of its roses did the shop sell that day?

_____

13. Bonnie's orange was cut into eighths. She ate $\frac{3}{8}$ of the orange and her friend ate $\frac{3}{8}$ of it. Did they eat the whole orange? Explain.

_____

14. Write and solve a fraction word problem of your own.

_____

_____

_____

_____

Add and Subtract Fractions With Like Denominators **237**

# Remembering

**Write the answers as quickly as you can.**

**1.** $30 \div 6 =$ _____       **2.** $49 \div 7 =$ _____       **3.** $32 \div 4 =$ _____

**4.** $36 \div 6 =$ _____       **5.** $72 \div 9 =$ _____       **6.** $25 \div 5 =$ _____

**7.** $24 \div 4 =$ _____       **8.** $40 \div 8 =$ _____       **9.** $54 \div 9 =$ _____

**Evaluate each expression.**

**10.**       $a = 9$          **11.**      $c = 2$          **12.**      $m = 3$
$(16 \div 2) + (a - 9)$      $3 \cdot (4 \div c)$         $(7 + m) \cdot (48 \div 4)$

**Solve.**                                       *Show your work.*

**13.** There are 157 students in the fourth grade. If they each donate 5 pennies to the book fund, how many pennies will they donate in all?

_____

**14.** In one week, Mary practiced the piano for 358 minutes. About how many minutes did she practice each day of the week? Explain.

_____

_____

**Name each triangle by its sides and then by its angles.**

**15.** 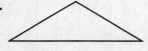                **16.**

_____         _____

**17.**                 **18.**

_____         _____

# Homework

**Write the equivalent improper fraction.**

**1.** $6\frac{2}{5} =$ _____  **2.** $2\frac{3}{8} =$ _____  **3.** $4\frac{6}{7} =$ _____  **4.** $8\frac{1}{3} =$ _____

**5.** $3\frac{7}{10} =$ _____  **6.** $5\frac{5}{6} =$ _____  **7.** $7\frac{3}{4} =$ _____  **8.** $1\frac{4}{9} =$ _____

**Write the equivalent mixed number.**

**9.** $\frac{50}{7} =$ _____  **10.** $\frac{16}{10} =$ _____  **11.** $\frac{23}{4} =$ _____  **12.** $\frac{50}{5} =$ _____

**13.** $\frac{21}{8} =$ _____  **14.** $\frac{11}{3} =$ _____  **15.** $\frac{60}{9} =$ _____  **16.** $\frac{23}{5} =$ _____

**Solve.**

*Show your work.*

**17.** Castor brought $6\frac{3}{4}$ small carrot cakes to share with the 26 students in his class. Did Castor bring enough for each student to have $\frac{1}{4}$ of a cake? Explain your thinking.

_____

_____

**18.** Claire cut some apples into eighths. She and her friends ate all but 17 pieces. How many whole apples and parts of apples did she have left over? Tell how you know.

_____

_____

**19.** Write and solve a fraction word problem of your own.

_____

_____

_____

_____

_____

**Name** _____ **Date** _____

# Remembering

**Multiply.**

1. $4 \times 4 =$ _____
2. $9 \times 6 =$ _____
3. $8 \times 3 =$ _____

4. $8 \times 7 =$ _____
5. $6 \times 3 =$ _____
6. $9 \times 8 =$ _____

7. $8 \times 6 =$ _____
8. $7 \times 4 =$ _____
9. $3 \times 7 =$ _____

**Divide.**

10. $5\overline{)96}$
11. $2\overline{)47}$
12. $8\overline{)609}$
13. $6\overline{)6,034}$

14. $3\overline{)84}$
15. $8\overline{)49}$
16. $7\overline{)298}$
17. $9\overline{)5,307}$

**Write the name of each triangle based on its sides. Then find the area and perimeter.**

18.

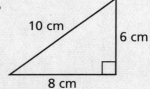

Name: _____

Area: _____

Perimeter: _____

19.

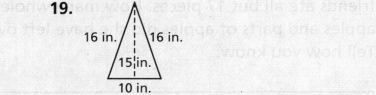

Name: _____

Area: _____

Perimeter: _____

**Write *P* for each prime and *C* for each composite number.**

20. 9 _____
21. 15 _____
22. 38 _____
23. 109 _____

**On separate paper, graph the points shown in the table.**

24.

| x | 1 | 2 | 3 | 4 | 6 |
|---|---|---|---|---|---|
| y | 3 | 4 | 5 | 6 | 8 |

Mixed Numbers and Improper Fractions

# Homework

## Add.

**1.** $3\frac{2}{6}$
  $+\ 6\frac{3}{6}$
_____

**2.** $8\frac{5}{10}$
  $+\ 9\frac{6}{10}$
_____

**3.** $7\frac{3}{4}$
  $+\ 4\frac{2}{4}$
_____

**4.** $1\frac{5}{9}$
  $+\ 5\frac{7}{9}$
_____

## Subtract.

**5.** $7\frac{2}{3}$
  $-\ 3\frac{1}{3}$
_____

**6.** $8\frac{2}{7}$
  $-\ 5\frac{5}{7}$
_____

**7.** $6\frac{1}{4}$
  $-\ 2\frac{3}{4}$
_____

**8.** $9\frac{1}{8}$
  $-\ 4\frac{5}{8}$
_____

## Add or subtract.

**9.** $\frac{1}{4} + \frac{7}{4} =$ _____

**10.** $\frac{3}{8} + \frac{6}{8} =$ _____

**11.** $\frac{9}{6} - \frac{8}{6} =$ _____

**12.** $\frac{5}{9} + \frac{6}{9} =$ _____

**13.** $\frac{9}{2} - \frac{6}{2} =$ _____

**14.** $\frac{5}{10} - \frac{2}{10} =$ _____

**15.** $\frac{2}{5} + \frac{4}{5} =$ _____

**16.** $\frac{8}{7} - \frac{3}{7} =$ _____

**17.** $\frac{7}{3} - \frac{2}{3} =$ _____

**18.** Write and solve a mixed number word problem.

_____

_____

_____

_____

_____

_____

_____

_____

_____

**Name** _____      **Date** _____

# Remembering

**Solve.**

**1.** 653 + 15,710 = _____

**2.** 85,132 − 6,409 = _____

**3.** 67 × 45 = _____

**4.** 784 ÷ 4 = _____

**5.** 8,147 + 54,479 = _____

**6.** 81,656 − 1,639 = _____

**7.** 39 × 76 = _____

**8.** 8,931 ÷ 6 = _____

**9.** 32,910 + 2,319 = _____

**10.** 65,325 − 8,607 = _____

**11.** 82 × 61 = _____

**12.** 9,424 ÷ 9 = _____

**Solve.**                                     *Show your work.*

**13.** The school baseball team played 56 games. They scored a mean (average) of 4 runs in each game. How many runs did they score in all?

_____

**14.** Matt collects football cards. His album holds 9 cards on each page. If he has 125 cards for his album, what is the greatest number of pages he can fill?

_____

**Find the area and perimeter of each triangle.**

**15.**
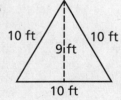

Area: _____

Perimeter: _____

**16.**
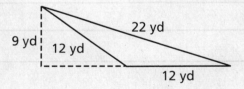

Area: _____

Perimeter: _____

**Solve for the variable in each equation.**

**17.** $r ÷ 5 = 35$

$r =$ _____

**18.** $p − 4 = 23$

$p =$ _____

**19.** $9w = 36$

$w =$ _____

Add and Subtract Mixed Numbers With Like Denominators

**Name** _____  **Date** _____

# Homework

## Insert > or < to make a true statement.

1. $\frac{2}{3}$ ◯ $\frac{2}{4}$

2. $\frac{5}{8}$ ◯ $\frac{5}{7}$

3. $\frac{3}{5}$ ◯ $\frac{3}{6}$

4. $\frac{7}{9}$ ◯ $\frac{8}{9}$

5. $\frac{5}{11}$ ◯ $\frac{6}{11}$

6. $\frac{4}{7}$ ◯ $\frac{3}{7}$

## Write each mixed number as an improper fraction.

7. $6\frac{5}{8} =$

8. $2\frac{1}{4} =$

9. $8\frac{3}{10} =$

10. $4\frac{2}{6} =$

## Write each improper fraction as a mixed number.

11. $\frac{26}{3} =$

12. $\frac{47}{7} =$

13. $\frac{59}{9} =$

14. $\frac{44}{5} =$

## Add or subtract.

15. $\frac{2}{3} + \frac{2}{3} =$

16. $\frac{4}{10} + \frac{12}{10} =$

17. $\frac{5}{7} - \frac{3}{7} =$

18. $1\frac{3}{9} + \frac{7}{9} =$

19. $\frac{3}{4} + 3\frac{3}{4} =$

20. $2\frac{4}{15} - \frac{10}{15} =$

21. $\frac{6}{12} + \frac{5}{12} =$

22. $\frac{15}{20} - \frac{6}{20} =$

23. $3\frac{3}{5} - 3\frac{1}{5} =$

24. $\frac{3}{6} + 2\frac{6}{6} =$

25. $2\frac{7}{8} - 1\frac{2}{8} =$

26. $1\frac{8}{11} - \frac{10}{11} =$

**Name** _____ **Date** _____

# Remembering

**Solve these problems about Mellie's Deli sandwiches.**

## Mellie's Deli

Regular (serves 2) _____ $3.00
Friendship (serves 4) _____ $5.00
Super (serves 10) _____ $12.00
Magna (serves 18) _____ $20.00

1. Suppose 5 friends each want 1 serving of a sandwich. How many Regular sandwiches will they need? If they ordered Friendship sandwiches, how many would they need?

   _____

   _____

2. Ten friends go to Mellie's after a soccer game and order 3 Friendship sandwiches. If each person has 1 sandwich serving, what fraction of the Friendship sandwiches will they eat all together?

   _____

3. There will be 25 people at Morey's graduation party. Should Morey order Super or Magna sandwiches? Explain your thinking.

   _____

   _____

   _____

4. Draw and label a right angle, an acute angle, and an obtuse angle.

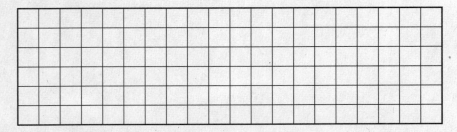

Practice With Fractions

# Homework

**Shade the fraction bar to show the fraction of items sold. Group the unit fractions to form an equivalent fraction in simplest form. Show your work numerically.**

1. The manager of Fantasy Flowers made 8 bouquets of wild flowers. By noon, she sold 2 of the bouquets. What fraction did she sell?

| $\frac{1}{8}$ | $\frac{1}{8}$ | $\frac{1}{8}$ | $\frac{1}{8}$ | $\frac{1}{8}$ | $\frac{1}{8}$ | $\frac{1}{8}$ | $\frac{1}{8}$ |
|---|---|---|---|---|---|---|---|

Group size: _____     Fraction of bouquets sold: $\frac{2 \div}{8 \div} =$ _____

2. A car dealer had 12 red cars on his lot at the beginning of the month. The first week he sold 8 of them. What fraction did he sell that week?

| $\frac{1}{12}$ | $\frac{1}{12}$ | $\frac{1}{12}$ | $\frac{1}{12}$ | $\frac{1}{12}$ | $\frac{1}{12}$ | $\frac{1}{12}$ | $\frac{1}{12}$ | $\frac{1}{12}$ | $\frac{1}{12}$ | $\frac{1}{12}$ | $\frac{1}{12}$ |
|---|---|---|---|---|---|---|---|---|---|---|---|

Group size: _____     Fraction of red cars sold: $\frac{8 \div}{12 \div} =$ _____

3. A music store received 10 copies of a new CD. They sold 6 of them in the first hour. What fraction did the store sell in the first hour?

| $\frac{1}{10}$ | $\frac{1}{10}$ | $\frac{1}{10}$ | $\frac{1}{10}$ | $\frac{1}{10}$ | $\frac{1}{10}$ | $\frac{1}{10}$ | $\frac{1}{10}$ | $\frac{1}{10}$ | $\frac{1}{10}$ |
|---|---|---|---|---|---|---|---|---|---|

Group size: _____     Fraction of CDs sold: $\frac{6 \div}{10 \div} =$ _____

**Simplify each fraction.**

4. $\frac{3 \div}{24 \div} =$ _____          5. $\frac{12 \div}{16 \div} =$ _____

6. $\frac{21 \div}{49 \div} =$ _____          7. $\frac{18 \div}{45 \div} =$ _____

**Name** _____    **Date** _____

# Remembering

Two years ago, the village of Jefferson Square opened a new park. The bar graph below shows how many people visited the new park during its first two summers.

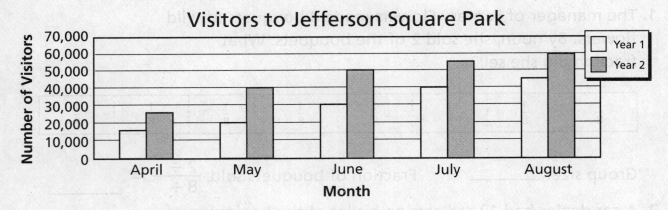

1. About how many people visited the new park in April of Year 1? _____

2. About how many people visited the new park in April of Year 2? _____

3. About how many more people visited the new park in April of Year 2 than in April of Year 1? _____

4. About how many times as many people visited the new park in May of Year 2 than in May of Year 1? _____

5. About how many times as many people visited the new park in August of Year 2 than in May of Year 1? _____

**Solve.**

6. What is the side length of a square with an area of 81 square inches? _____

7. How many one-meter squares fit inside a square with an area of 36 square meters? _____

8. What is the side length of a square with area 49 square feet? _____

Simplify Fractions

**Find a common denominator and then add.**

1. $\frac{1}{4} + \frac{2}{3} =$ _____

| $\frac{1}{4}$ | | | | $\frac{1}{4}$ | | | | $\frac{1}{4}$ | | | | $\frac{1}{4}$ |
|---|---|---|---|---|---|---|---|---|---|---|---|---|
| $\frac{1}{12}$ | $\frac{1}{12}$ | $\frac{1}{12}$ | $\frac{1}{12}$ | $\frac{1}{12}$ | $\frac{1}{12}$ | $\frac{1}{12}$ | $\frac{1}{12}$ | $\frac{1}{12}$ | $\frac{1}{12}$ | $\frac{1}{12}$ | $\frac{1}{12}$ | |
| $\frac{1}{3}$ | | | | $\frac{1}{3}$ | | | | $\frac{1}{3}$ | | | | |

**Write the equivalent fraction shown by the second shape.
Then fill in the blanks to complete the sentences in
exercises 3 and 4.**

2.

$\frac{1}{3} =$ _____

3. The shaded part of the first shape is divided into _____
equal parts to make the shaded parts of the second shape.

4. The numerator and denominator of $\frac{1}{3}$ is multiplied by
_____ to make the equivalent fraction.

**Find a common denominator and add. Do not change
improper fractions to mixed numbers.**

5. $\frac{1}{6} + \frac{3}{5} =$

6. $\frac{3}{8} + \frac{3}{4} =$

7. $\frac{1}{4} + \frac{1}{6} =$

8. $\frac{5}{7} + \frac{2}{3} =$

9. $\frac{2}{3} + \frac{1}{2} =$

10. $\frac{2}{5} + \frac{7}{10} =$

# Remembering

**Name** _____ **Date** _____

**Solve. Use a separate sheet of paper if necessary.**

1. 4)95 $\qquad$ 2. 6)178 $\qquad$ 3. 4)296 $\qquad$ 4. 3)7,608

5. $37 \times 2 =$ ___ 6. $95 \times 8 =$ ___ 7. $420 \times 5 =$ ___ 8. $237 \times 6 =$ ___

9. $4a + 2 = 10$ 10. $2c - 7 = 17$ 11. $3m + 9 = 36$

$a =$ _____ $c =$ _____ $m =$ _____

12. Which two figures look congruent? Explain how you know.

_____

_____

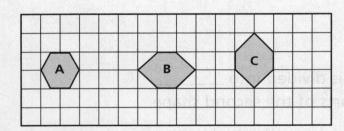

**Every year, Joey and Jane plant a vegetable garden together.**
**Solve these problems about their gardening.**

13. The first day of the gardening season, Joey planted $\frac{2}{5}$ of
the garden and Jane planted $\frac{1}{3}$. What fraction of their
garden did they plant that day?

_____

14. Joey and Jane have seeds to plant in their garden. Joey
planted $\frac{3}{8}$ and Jane planted $\frac{2}{6}$ of their seeds. What total
fraction of their seeds did Joey and Jane plant in all?

_____

Add Fractions With Unlike Denominators

**Name** _____ **Date** _____

# Homework

For each pair of fractions, find equivalent fractions with a common denominator. Then compare, add, and subtract the fractions.

| Sample. | Find equivalent fractions. | Compare. |
|---|---|---|
| $\dfrac{5}{7}$  $\dfrac{2}{3}$ | $\dfrac{5 \times 3}{7 \times 3} = \dfrac{15}{21}$  $\dfrac{2 \times 7}{3 \times 7} = \dfrac{14}{21}$ | $\dfrac{5}{7} > \dfrac{2}{3}$ |

**Add.**

$$\dfrac{15}{21} + \dfrac{14}{21} = \dfrac{15 + 14}{21} = \dfrac{29}{21}$$

**Subtract.**

$$\dfrac{15}{21} - \dfrac{14}{21} = \dfrac{15 - 14}{21} = \dfrac{1}{21}$$

**1.** $\dfrac{2}{5}$   $\dfrac{1}{6}$ _____

**2.** $\dfrac{5}{6}$   $\dfrac{3}{4}$ _____

**3.** $\dfrac{5}{6}$   $\dfrac{2}{3}$ _____

**Solve.**

*Show your work.*

**4.** Marlon ate $\dfrac{1}{3}$ of the banana. His sister ate $\dfrac{4}{9}$ of the banana. How much of the banana did they eat in all?

_____

**5.** A glass held $\dfrac{2}{5}$ cup of water. Carlo poured out $\dfrac{3}{8}$ cup. How much water was left in the glass?

_____

**6.** Craig and Nora are taking paper to the recycling center. Craig has $\dfrac{5}{7}$ pound of paper. Nora has $\dfrac{2}{3}$ pound of paper. Who is taking less paper to the recycling center? _____

How much less? _____

**Find equivalent fractions.**

**7.** $\dfrac{2}{3} = \dfrac{}{15}$      **8.** $\dfrac{4}{7} = \dfrac{}{21}$      **9.** $\dfrac{24}{32} = \dfrac{}{4}$      **10.** $\dfrac{70}{90} = \dfrac{}{9}$

# Remembering

Name _____  Date _____

**Find the simplest equivalent fraction.**

1. $\frac{20}{30} =$ _____

2. $\frac{18}{42} =$ _____

3. $\frac{10}{18} =$ _____

4. $\frac{18}{24} =$ _____

5. $\frac{18}{36} =$ _____

6. $\frac{42}{48} =$ _____

7. $\frac{10}{24} =$ _____

8. $\frac{36}{48} =$ _____

9. $\frac{20}{80} =$ _____

10. $\frac{36}{45} =$ _____

11. $\frac{24}{54} =$ _____

12. $\frac{28}{35} =$ _____

**Tell how much time has passed between the times shown on each pair of clocks. Be sure to pay attention to the AM and PM markings on the clocks.**

13.

_____

14.

_____

15.

_____

16.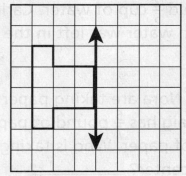

_____

**Reflect each figure across the given line.**

17.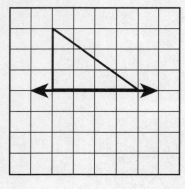

18.

Compare and Subtract Fractions With Unlike Denominators

# Homework

## Insert <, >, or = to make a true statement

1. $\dfrac{5}{6}$ ◯ $\dfrac{9}{10}$          2. $\dfrac{2}{8}$ ◯ $\dfrac{4}{16}$          3. $\dfrac{7}{5}$ ◯ $\dfrac{5}{3}$

4. $\dfrac{6}{7}$ ◯ $\dfrac{4}{6}$          5. $\dfrac{7}{8}$ ◯ $\dfrac{10}{12}$          6. $\dfrac{3}{4}$ ◯ $\dfrac{8}{12}$

## Add or subtract.

7. $\dfrac{3}{6} + \dfrac{4}{8} =$                      8. $\dfrac{2}{4} + \dfrac{9}{10} =$

9. $\dfrac{4}{5} - \dfrac{5}{7} =$                    10. $\dfrac{2}{5} + \dfrac{2}{9} =$

11. $\dfrac{6}{7} + \dfrac{1}{3} =$                   12. $\dfrac{4}{9} - \dfrac{1}{5} =$

13. $\dfrac{1}{4} + \dfrac{2}{7} =$                   14. $\dfrac{7}{9} - \dfrac{2}{6} =$

15. $\dfrac{7}{8} - \dfrac{3}{4} =$                   16. $\dfrac{1}{2} + \dfrac{7}{10} =$

17. $\dfrac{5}{8} - \dfrac{3}{5} =$                   18. $\dfrac{5}{6} - \dfrac{4}{10} =$

## Find the simplest equivalent fraction.

19. $\dfrac{20}{30} =$ _____      20. $\dfrac{18}{42} =$ _____      21. $\dfrac{10}{18} =$ _____

22. $\dfrac{18}{24} =$ _____      23. $\dfrac{18}{36} =$ _____      24. $\dfrac{42}{48} =$ _____

25. $\dfrac{10}{24} =$ _____      26. $\dfrac{36}{48} =$ _____      27. $\dfrac{21}{28} =$ _____

**Name** _____  **Date** _____

# Remembering

**Write each mixed number as an improper fraction.**

**1.** $2\frac{2}{15} = \frac{}{15}$

**2.** $1\frac{3}{4} = \frac{}{4}$

**3.** $6\frac{7}{10} = \frac{}{10}$

**4.** $5\frac{1}{2} = \frac{}{2}$

**5.** $3\frac{5}{8} = \frac{}{8}$

**6.** $4\frac{5}{6} = \frac{}{6}$

**Write each improper fraction as a mixed number.**

**7.** $\frac{21}{12} = $ _____

**8.** $\frac{14}{3} = $ _____

**9.** $\frac{31}{9} = $ _____

**10.** $\frac{45}{7} = $ _____

**11.** $\frac{44}{20} = $ _____

**12.** $\frac{28}{5} = $ _____

*Show your work.*

**The Fin and Fur Pet Shop has 35 puppies ready for adoption. Solve each problem about the puppies.**

**13.** Twenty of the puppies are housebroken. What fraction are housebroken?

_____

**14.** If $\frac{3}{5}$ of the puppies are terriers, what fraction are not terriers?

_____

**15.** Maggie walked $\frac{2}{7}$ of the puppies. Josh walked $\frac{1}{5}$ of the puppies. What fraction of the puppies did they walk altogether?

_____

**16.** Jing fed $\frac{3}{7}$ of the puppies. Theo fed $\frac{2}{5}$ of the puppies. Who fed fewer puppies? How many fewer?

_____

**Complete each row.**

| | Millimeters | Centimeters | Decimeters | Meters |
|---|---|---|---|---|
| **17.** | 40 | 4 | _____ | 0.04 |
| **18.** | _____ | 30 | 3 | 0.3 |
| **19.** | 7,500 | 750 | 75 | _____ |

Practice With Unlike Denominators

A bucket of 100 marbles contains 10 green marbles, 20 purple marbles, 30 yellow marbles, and 40 red marbles. Harry takes one marble out of the bucket without looking.

**1.** Is Harry's marble more likely to be red or yellow? Explain.

_____

_____

**2.** What is the probability that Harry's marble is purple?

_____

_____

**3.** What is the probability that Harry's marble is purple or yellow? Explain.

_____

_____

**4.** What is the probability that Harry's marble is white? Explain.

_____

_____

**5.** Suppose Harry takes out all of the green marbles and then chooses a marble. What is the probability he will get a purple marble?

_____

**6.** Suppose Harry adds 10 more red marbles to the bucket. What is the probability he will get a purple marble?

_____

**7.** Write and solve your own probability problem about Harry's bucket of marbles.

_____

_____

_____

**Suppose you spin the spinner at the right one time.**

**8.** What is the probability you will win? _____

**9.** What is the probability you will lose? _____

**10.** What is the probability you will not win? _____

# Remembering

**Write the equivalent improper fraction.**

**1.** $8\frac{7}{8} = $ _____

**2.** $9\frac{2}{3} = $ _____

**3.** $7\frac{3}{10} = $ _____

**4.** $3\frac{1}{4} = $ _____

**5.** $4\frac{2}{5} = $ _____

**6.** $6\frac{5}{9} = $ _____

**7.** $2\frac{5}{6} = $ _____

**8.** $5\frac{4}{7} = $ _____

**Write the equivalent mixed number.**

**9.** $\frac{50}{9} = $ _____

**10.** $\frac{25}{3} = $ _____

**11.** $\frac{22}{6} = $ _____

**12.** $\frac{52}{8} = $ _____

**13.** $\frac{33}{7} = $ _____

**14.** $\frac{18}{5} = $ _____

**15.** $\frac{46}{10} = $ _____

**16.** $\frac{35}{4} = $ _____

**Solve.**

*Show your work.*

**17.** Kam cut a melon into eighths. Her four brothers each ate one piece. What fraction of the melon did they eat in all?

_____

**18.** Mel cut a pizza into 6 equal pieces. She and her three friends each ate one piece. What fraction of the pizza did they eat?

_____

**Complete each function table. Then write the rule.**

**19.**

| x | y |
|---|---|
| 2 | 8 |
| 3 | 12 |
| 4 | 16 |
| 5 |   |
| 6 |   |
| 7 |   |

$y = $ _____

**20.**

| x | y |
|---|---|
| 1 | 5 |
| 2 | 7 |
| 3 | 9 |
| 4 |   |
| 5 |   |
| 6 |   |

$y = $ _____

Discover Probability

Name _____     Date _____

Tyler asked each classmate for the total number of hours he or she reads in one week. The amounts they named are shown in the frequency table below.

| Number of Reading Hours | Number of Students |
|:---:|:---:|
| 5 | 5 |
| 6 | 3 |
| 7 | 4 |
| 8 | 5 |
| 9 | 3 |
| 10 | 7 |

**1.** Make a line plot of the data.

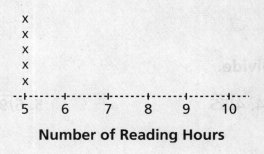

**Number of Reading Hours**

**2.** How many students did Tyler ask in all? Explain how you know.

_____

**3.** The number of hours Tyler reads in a week is equal to the median of the data.
Tyler reads _____ hours in a week.

**4.** The number of hours Layla reads in a week is equal to the range of the data.
Layla reads _____ hours in a week.

**5.** Tyler asked one more student for the number of hours he read in one week. This student read 8 hours in one week. If Tyler includes this information on his frequency table and line plot, will it change the median of the data? Explain your choice.

_____

_____

# Remembering

**Multiply.**

**1.** 56 × 8 = _____

**2.** 704 × 3 = _____

**3.** 82 × 35 = _____

**Divide.**

**4.** 4)‾55‾

**5.** 6)‾996‾

**6.** 3)‾2,807‾

**Solve.**

**7.** The cost to make a belt is $5.25 for the buckle plus
$0.75 for every inch of leather used. Let *a* represent
the number of inches of leather used. Explain how
to change the expression $5.25 – $0.75*a* to represent
the cost to make a belt.

_____

_____

**8.** Describe the **two** transformations that were used to move
the figure to its new location.

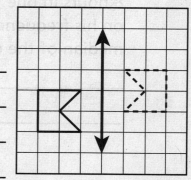

_____

_____

_____

_____

# Homework

**Multiply.**

**1.** $3 \times \frac{1}{4} =$ _____

**2.** $5 \times \frac{1}{3} =$ _____

**3.** $4 \times \frac{1}{6} =$ _____

**4.** $7 \times \frac{1}{7} =$ _____

**5.** $2 \times \frac{1}{8} =$ _____

**6.** $3 \times \frac{1}{10} =$ _____

**7.** $2 \times \frac{3}{4} =$ _____

**8.** $12 \times \frac{2}{3} =$ _____

**9.** $12 \times \frac{5}{6} =$ _____

**10.** $3 \times \frac{2}{7} =$ _____

**11.** $24 \times \frac{5}{8} =$ _____

**12.** $8 \times \frac{3}{10} =$ _____

**13.** $20 \times \frac{3}{5} =$ _____

**14.** $9 \times \frac{5}{9} =$ _____

**15.** $10 \times \frac{7}{12} =$ _____

**Solve.**

*Show your work.*

**16.** Manuel eats $\frac{1}{8}$ of a melon for a snack each day. How much melon does he eat in five days?

_____

**17.** Shannen collects paper for recycling. If she collects $\frac{1}{3}$ of a pound of paper each week, how much paper will she collect in 4 weeks?

_____

**18.** Aisha is unpacking boxes. If it takes $\frac{3}{4}$ hour to unpack each box, how long will it take her to unpack 6 boxes?

_____

**19.** Mrs. Suarez cut a pizza into 8 equal pieces. Each person in her family ate 2 pieces. If there are 3 people in her family, what fraction of the pizza did they eat altogether?

_____

**20.** Hailey is knitting a scarf. Each half hour, she adds $\frac{3}{7}$ of an inch to the scarf's length. How much length will she add to the scarf in 6 hours?

_____

# Remembering

**Insert > or < to make each statement true.**

1. $\frac{4}{6}$ ◯ $\frac{4}{5}$

2. $\frac{8}{9}$ ◯ $\frac{7}{9}$

3. $\frac{10}{15}$ ◯ $\frac{10}{16}$

4. $\frac{5}{7}$ ◯ $\frac{6}{7}$

5. $\frac{9}{10}$ ◯ $\frac{9}{12}$

6. $\frac{2}{9}$ ◯ $\frac{3}{9}$

**Solve.**                                          *Show your work.*

7. Jerome sold $\frac{1}{4}$ of his coin collection one weekend.
   The next weekend he sold another $\frac{2}{5}$ of his
   collection. What fraction of his collection did
   he sell? _____

8. Tom's spent $\frac{2}{4}$ of his allowance at the video
   arcade. What fraction of his allowance does he
   have left? _____

**Divide.**

9. $5\overline{)16}$

10. $6\overline{)781}$

11. $9\overline{)7,904}$

12. $3\overline{)7,681}$

**Use Figures A, B, and C for Exercises 13 and 14.**

**Figure A**

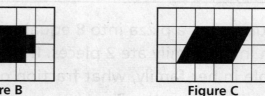

**Figure B**                    **Figure C**

13. List the figures that have line symmetry.

_____

14. List the figures that have rotational symmetry.
    Give the degree of rotation for each figure.

_____

Multiply a Fraction by a Whole Number

**Name** _____ **Date** _____

# Homework

The librarian sorted social studies books into eight equal piles.

  Two of the piles were books about history.

  Three of the piles were books about geography.

  Two of the piles were books about people.

  The books in the last pile were about other topics.

Then the librarian made a circle graph about the piles.

1. Write the book topic for each section of the circle graph.

   Section A: _____

   Section B: _____

   Section C: _____

   Section D: _____

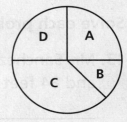

2. Is there another possible answer for problem 1? Explain.

   _____

**Solve.**

3. $\frac{1}{4} \times 20 =$ _____

4. $\frac{1}{3} \times 18 =$ _____

5. $\frac{1}{8} \times 7 =$ _____

6. $\frac{7}{10} \times 80 =$ _____

7. $\frac{3}{5} \times 30 =$ _____

8. $\frac{4}{9} \times 54 =$ _____

**Solve each problem.**

9. David exercised for 45 minutes. He jumped rope for $\frac{1}{9}$ of the time. How many minutes did he jump rope?

   _____

10. Marlon collected 36 cans for recycling. He put $\frac{3}{4}$ of the cans in a bag to take to the recycling center. How many cans did he put in the bag?

   _____

11. Tara earned $25 from babysitting. She put $\frac{2}{5}$ of the money into a savings account. How much money did she put in her savings account?

   _____

12. Tony got $\frac{5}{6}$ of the problems on the math test correct. There were 42 problems on the test. How many problems did Tony get wrong?

   _____

**Name** _____ **Date** _____

# Remembering

**Add or subtract.**

1. $\frac{2}{8} + \frac{3}{8} =$

2. $\frac{1}{6} + \frac{3}{6} =$

3. $\frac{4}{9} + \frac{2}{9} =$

4. $\frac{4}{7} - \frac{1}{7} =$

5. $\frac{5}{6} - \frac{2}{6} =$

6. $\frac{7}{9} - \frac{3}{9} =$

7. $\frac{1}{9} + \frac{2}{3} =$

8. $\frac{5}{6} + \frac{2}{5} =$

9. $\frac{3}{8} + \frac{2}{7} =$

10. $\frac{3}{4} - \frac{1}{8} =$

11. $\frac{4}{7} - \frac{1}{2} =$

12. $\frac{4}{5} - \frac{2}{3} =$

**Solve each problem.**

*Show your work.*

13. Mr. Sanchez planted a garden that is 35 feet wide and 84 feet long. What is the area of the garden?

_____

14. Clair packed 342 books into boxes. She put 9 books in each box. How many boxes did she use?

_____

15. Lincoln Middle School put on a play as a fundraiser. Tickets to the play cost $8. If 231 people attended the play, how much money did they raise?

_____

**Find the perimeter and area of each figure.**

16.

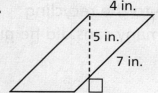

Perimeter: _____

Area: _____

17.

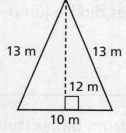

Perimeter: _____

Area: _____

**Simplify each expression.**

18. $3a + 10$ when $a = 7$ _____

19. $48 \div (4 + c)$ when $c = 8$ _____

Fractions of Whole Numbers

# Homework

The graph below shows the number of goals scored last season by five players on one soccer team.

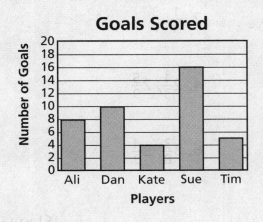

**Goals Scored**

**Complete each comparison sentence.**

**1.** Ali scored _____ as many goals as Sue scored.

Sue scored _____ times as many goals as Ali scored.

**2.** Kate scored _____ as many goals as Sue scored.

Sue scored _____ times as many goals as Kate scored.

**3.** Dan scored _____ times as many goals as Tim scored.

Tim scored _____ as many goals as Dan scored.

**Solve. Draw comparison bars if you need to.**     *Show your work.*

**4.** While on vacation, Holly sent 17 postcards to her friends. Megan sent 3 times as many postcards as Holly. How many postcards did Megan send?

_____

**5.** Max did 19 sit-ups. This is $\frac{1}{7}$ as many sit-ups as Isabel did. How many sit-ups did Isabel do?

_____

# Remembering

**Compare each pair of numbers. Then add the numbers and subtract the smaller number from the larger number.**

1. $\frac{8}{9}$, $\frac{1}{4}$

2. $\frac{1}{4}$, $\frac{3}{7}$

3. $\frac{6}{2}$, $\frac{8}{3}$

4. $2\frac{1}{3}$, $2\frac{5}{9}$

5. $1\frac{2}{7}$, $2\frac{1}{4}$

6. $3\frac{3}{8}$, $3\frac{4}{9}$

**Solve each problem.**                          *Show your work.*

7. Geneva has 35 trading cards. One-seventh of them are baseball cards. How many baseball cards does Geneva have? _____

8. Ming had 64 newspapers to deliver. She delivered $\frac{7}{8}$ of the newspapers so far. How many papers does she still have left to deliver? _____

9. The school store orders pencils in boxes of 24 per box. They sell $3\frac{3}{8}$ boxes of pencils one week. How many pencils is this? _____

**Name each figure.**

10.

_____

11.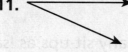

_____

12.

_____

# Homework

**Give two equivalent fractions or mixed numbers for each lettered dot. Fractions can be improper.**

1.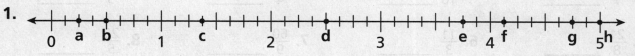

a. _____   b. _____   c. _____   d. _____

e. _____   f. _____   g. _____   h. _____

2.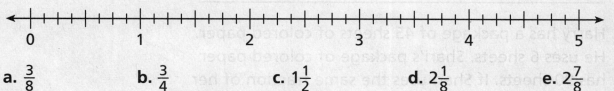

a. _____   b. _____   c. _____

d. _____   e. _____   f. _____

3. Mark and label the point for each fraction or mixed number with its letter.

```
←|++++|++++|++++|++++|++++|→
 0    1    2    3    4    5
```

a. $\frac{3}{8}$        b. $\frac{3}{4}$        c. $1\frac{1}{2}$        d. $2\frac{1}{8}$        e. $2\frac{7}{8}$

f. $3\frac{1}{4}$        g. $3\frac{5}{8}$        h. $4\frac{2}{4}$        i. $4\frac{6}{8}$        j. $4\frac{7}{8}$

4. Draw your own number line and mark some points and label them.

**Name** _____ **Date** _____

# Remembering

**Find the equivalent mixed number.**

1. $\frac{50}{7}$ _____

2. $\frac{16}{10}$ _____

3. $\frac{23}{4}$ _____

4. $\frac{50}{5}$ _____

5. $\frac{21}{8}$ _____

6. $\frac{11}{3}$ _____

7. $\frac{60}{9}$ _____

8. $\frac{23}{5}$ _____

**Write the equivalent improper fraction.**

9. $6\frac{2}{5}$ _____

10. $2\frac{3}{8}$ _____

11. $4\frac{6}{7}$ _____

12. $8\frac{1}{3}$ _____

13. $3\frac{7}{10}$ _____

14. $5\frac{5}{6}$ _____

15. $7\frac{3}{4}$ _____

16. $1\frac{4}{9}$ _____

**Solve each problem.**

*Show your work.*

17. The fruit market buys oranges in boxes of 48 and apples in boxes of 36. They sold $\frac{1}{3}$ of a box of oranges and $\frac{1}{9}$ of a box of apples. How many oranges did they sell? How many apples did they sell? How many pieces of fruit did they sell in all?

_____

_____

18. Harry has a package of 45 sheets of colored paper. He uses 6 sheets. Shari's package of colored paper has 90 sheets. If Shari uses the same fraction of her package as Harry used of his, how many sheets will she use?

_____

**Label each angle as right, acute, or obtuse.**

19.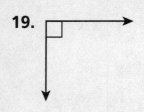

20.

21.

_____ _____ _____

Fractions on the Number Line

**Write >, <, or = to make each statement true.**

1. $\frac{5}{8}$ ◯ $\frac{1}{2}$

2. $\frac{2}{9}$ ◯ $\frac{1}{4}$

3. $\frac{2}{3}$ ◯ $\frac{3}{6}$

4. $\frac{5}{6}$ ◯ $\frac{7}{8}$

**Write the fractions in order from greatest to least.**

5. $\frac{2}{6}, \frac{2}{4}, \frac{2}{8}$ _____

6. $\frac{5}{10}, \frac{5}{9}, \frac{5}{7}$ _____

**Add or subtract.**

7. $\frac{2}{5} + \frac{1}{5} =$ _____

8. $\frac{7}{8} - \frac{5}{8} =$ _____

9. $\frac{2}{5} + \frac{5}{6} =$ _____

10. $\frac{3}{4} - \frac{1}{8} =$ _____

11. $7\frac{1}{4} + 3\frac{5}{7} =$ _____

12. $6\frac{1}{6} - 3\frac{2}{5} =$ _____

**Write the simplest equivalent fraction.**

13. $\frac{20}{40} =$ _____

14. $\frac{14}{42} =$ _____

15. $\frac{5}{30} =$ _____

16. $\frac{20}{28} =$ _____

17. $\frac{21}{35} =$ _____

18. $\frac{27}{36} =$ _____

**Multiply.**

19. $\frac{1}{8} \times 40 =$ _____

20. $30 \times \frac{5}{6} =$ _____

21. $\frac{3}{7} \times 42 =$ _____

22. $\frac{1}{5} \times 12 =$ _____

23. $27 \times \frac{1}{4} =$ _____

24. $\frac{2}{5} \times 12 =$ _____

# Remembering

**Solve each problem.**

1. Dottie walks 21 blocks to school each day. That is 3 times as many blocks as Jed walks. How many blocks does Jed walk?

   _____

2. A child's train ticket costs $7. That is $\frac{1}{4}$ as much as an adult's ticket. How much does an adult's train ticket cost?

   _____

Mr. Wong's class raised $72 to buy books for their class library.

3. Darnell earned $\frac{1}{6}$ of the money doing extra chores at home. How much did he earn?

   _____

4. Susanna and her sister had a bake sale, and earned $\frac{2}{9}$ of the money. How much did they earn?

   _____

5. Maria earned $\frac{1}{3}$ of the money helping neighborhood children with their homework. How much did Maria earn?

   _____

6. Describe how the figure was translated.

   _____

   _____

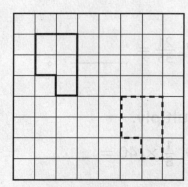

Practice With Fractions

**Name** _____     **Date** _____

# Homework

## 1. Connections

Chen ate $\frac{5}{6}$ of a pizza. Dave ate $\frac{5}{8}$ of the same size pizza. Who ate more pizza? Explain how you know?

_____

_____

_____

## 2. Reasoning and Proof

The numerator of a fraction less than one is greater than half of the denominator. Is the fraction closer to 1 or to 0? Use an example to support or disprove.

_____

_____

_____

## 3. Communication

Can a fraction that is in simplified form ever have an even number in the numerator and an even number in the denominator? Explain.

_____

_____

_____

## 4. Representation

Jason and his friends ordered 3 pizzas. They have eaten $1\frac{5}{8}$ pizzas. Draw a picture that shows how much pizza is left. Write a sentence or two that explains your drawing.

_____

_____

_____

# Remembering

**Find the equivalent mixed number.**

1. $\frac{40}{9}$ = _____

2. $\frac{25}{7}$ = _____

3. $\frac{32}{8}$ = _____

4. $\frac{17}{3}$ = _____

5. $\frac{30}{4}$ = _____

6. $\frac{47}{6}$ = _____

7. $\frac{23}{5}$ = _____

8. $\frac{17}{10}$ = _____

**Find the equivalent improper fraction.**

9. $4\frac{1}{3}$ = _____

10. $2\frac{5}{9}$ = _____

11. $5\frac{3}{5}$ = _____

12. $3\frac{6}{7}$ = _____

13. $7\frac{1}{4}$ = _____

14. $1\frac{5}{6}$ = _____

15. $2\frac{3}{10}$ = _____

16. $5\frac{3}{8}$ = _____

**Solve each problem.**                                    *Show your work.*

17. Maria bought a book for $5. The book was
$\frac{1}{3}$ the cost of another book she bought. What
is the cost of the other book?

_____

18. The stationary store has pencils that come in
boxes of 45 and pens that come in boxes of 48. The
store sold $\frac{1}{5}$ of a box of pencils and $\frac{1}{8}$ of a box
of pens. How many pencils did they sell?
How many pens did they sell?

_____

**Label each angle as right, acute, or obtuse.**

19.

20.

21.
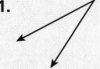

_____        _____        _____

Use Mathematical Processes

**Name each figure. Describe what makes each figure different from the others.**

1.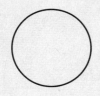

2.

3.

4.

_____    _____

_____    _____

_____    _____

_____

**Write the number of cubes in each stack.**

5.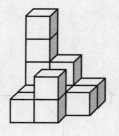

6.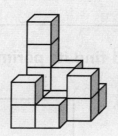

7.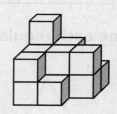

_____    _____    _____

**Can you fold each net to make a cube? Write *yes* or *no*. If necessary, test the nets by tracing them on paper and cutting them out and making a cube.**

8.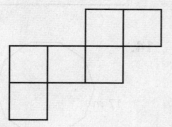

9.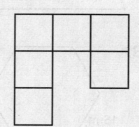

10.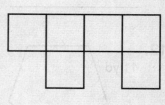

_____    _____    _____

**Name** _____ **Date** _____

# Remembering

**Solve.**

Show your work.

1. $1\frac{2}{3} + 2\frac{1}{3} =$ _____

2. $3\frac{4}{5} - 2\frac{1}{5} =$ _____

3. $2\frac{3}{8} + 2\frac{7}{8} =$ _____

4. $4\frac{1}{6} + 1\frac{5}{6} =$ _____

5. $1\frac{3}{10} + 2\frac{7}{10} =$ _____

6. $5\frac{1}{4} - 4\frac{3}{4} =$ _____

7. A DVD machine can duplicate one disc every 3 seconds. At this rate, how many discs can the machine duplicate in 1 hour?

   _____

8. A CD holds 80 minutes of music. If each song on the CD is an average of 3 minutes, about how many songs can fit on the CD?

   _____

**Name each regular polygon and find its perimeter.**

9.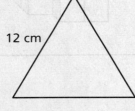

   12 cm

   _____

10.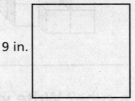

    9 in.

    _____

11.

    6 in.

    _____

12.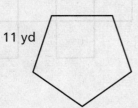

    11 yd

    _____

13.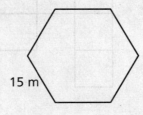

    15 m

    _____

14.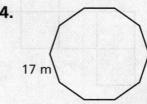

    17 m

    _____

Spheres and Cubes

# Homework

**Name the prisms that have these figures as their bases.**

1.

_____

2.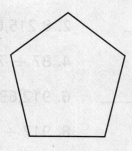

_____

3.

_____

4.

_____

5.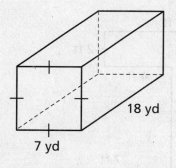

_____

6.

_____

**Find the surface area of each prism. Show your work.**
**Remember: A small mark ( – ) means that the edges are congruent.**

7.

18 yd

7 yd

_____

8.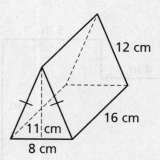

12 cm

16 cm

11 cm

8 cm

_____

**Name** _____  **Date** _____

# Remembering

**Complete each number sentence. Show your work on a separate sheet of paper.**

**1.** 1,326 + 456,106 = _____

**2.** 8,215,005 − 23,749 = _____

**3.** 7 × 634 = _____

**4.** 87 ÷ 7 = _____

**5.** 63,808 + 4,775,096 = _____

**6.** 912,634 − 8,856 = _____

**7.** 91 × 28 = _____

**8.** 917 ÷ 5 = _____

**9.** 536,697 + 14,194 = _____

**10.** 503,652 − 46,847 = _____

**11.** 18 × 39 = _____

**12.** 639 ÷ 9 = _____

**Find the perimeter of each regular polygon.**

**13.**
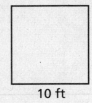
10 ft

_____

**14.**

7 ft

_____

**15.**
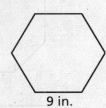
9 in.

**16.**

8 in.

**Find the perimeter and area of each figure. Show your work.**

**17.**
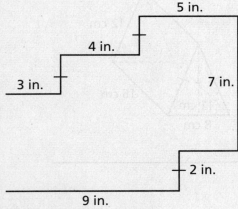

5 in.
4 in.
3 in.
7 in.
2 in.
9 in.

P = _____

A = _____

**18.**
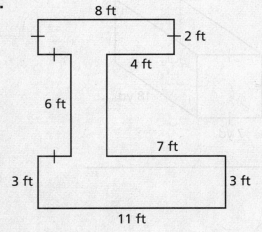

8 ft
2 ft
4 ft
6 ft
7 ft
3 ft
3 ft
11 ft

P = _____

A = _____

Prisms and Cylinders

# Homework

**Name each solid. Also name the base, where possible.**

1.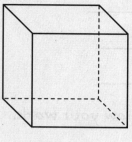

_____

_____

2.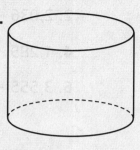

_____

_____

3.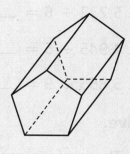

_____

_____

4.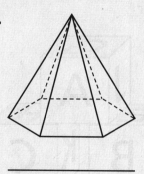

_____

_____

5.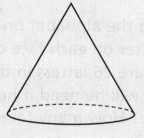

_____

_____

6.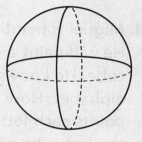

_____

_____

7. Describe one similarity and one difference among spheres, cones, and cylinders.

_____

_____

_____

_____

8. Describe one similarity and one difference among cubes, square prisms, and square pyramids.

_____

_____

_____

_____

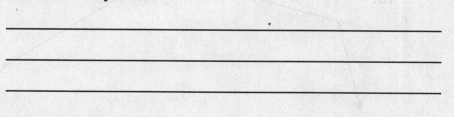

# Remembering

**Divide. Show your work on a separate sheet of paper.**

1. 5,232 ÷ 6 = _____

2. 2,036 ÷ 4 = _____

3. 4,945 ÷ 5 = _____

4. 1,285 ÷ 3 = _____

5. 5,855 ÷ 9 = _____

6. 3,555 ÷ 7 = _____

**Solve.**

*Show your work.*

7. The surface area of a cube is 1,950 sq cm. What is the area of each face of the cube?

_____

8. Miguel is painting letters of the alphabet on cubes. He will paint a different letter on each face of each cube. He knows that there are 26 letters in the alphabet. How many cubes will he need if he paints each letter only once? How many faces on the last cube will be empty?

_____

**Describe each figure using geometry language.**

9.

_____

10.

_____

11.

_____

12.

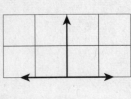

_____

13.

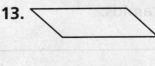

_____

14.

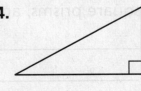

_____

Compare and Contrast Solids

# Homework

**Use the visual to fill in each blank.**

**1.** The shaded part of the whole represents:

$\frac{40}{100}$ = _____ of _____ equal parts and the decimal _____.

$\frac{4}{10}$ = _____ of _____ equal parts and the decimal _____.

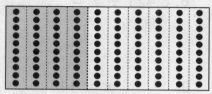

**2.** The shaded part of the whole represents:

$\frac{25}{100}$ = _____ of _____ equal parts $\frac{1}{4}$ = _____ of _____ equal parts and the decimal _____.

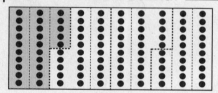

**3.** The shaded part of the whole represents:

$\frac{110}{100}$ = _____ of _____ equal parts $\frac{11}{10}$ = _____ of _____ equal parts

$1\frac{1}{10}$ = _____ whole and _____ of _____ equal parts and the decimal _____.

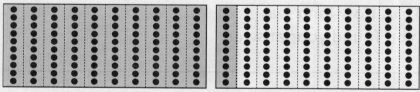

**Solve.**

**4.** Juan shaded a part of the whole. Four fractions represent the shaded part of the whole. List each fraction. Explain how each fraction relates to the shaded part of the whole.

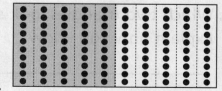

_____

_____

_____

**Multiply.**

**1.** $57 \times 8 =$ _____

**2.** $406 \times 7 =$ _____

**3.** $43 \times 27 =$ _____

**Divide.**

**4.** $59 \div 4 =$ _____

**5.** $904 \div 8 =$ _____

**6.** $8,421 \div 7 =$ _____

**Evaluate.**

**7.** $c = 3$

$(39 \div 3) + (3 - c)$

_____

**8.** $a = 5$

$(7 \cdot a) - (25 \div a)$

_____

**9.** $x = 11$

$(300 \div 3) - (13 + x)$

_____

**Solve.**

**10.** Mr. Williams bought 4 packs with 12 napkins in each pack. He gave 8 groups of students the same number of napkins. If each student in the group received only one napkin, how many students are in each group?

_____

**11.** The tour of the museum started at 11:45 A.M. The tour ended at 2:30 P.M. How long was the tour? Explain how you found your answer.

_____

_____

_____

**12.** Which two triangles look similar? Explain how you know.

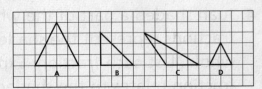

_____

_____

_____

Relate Fractions and Decimals

**Name** _____ **Date** _____

# Homework

Write a fraction and a decimal number to show what part of each bar is shaded.

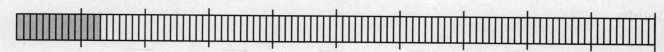

**1.** Fraction: _____ Decimal Number: _____

**2.** Fraction: _____ Decimal Number: _____

Write these amounts as decimal numbers.

**3.** 5 tenths _____ **4.** 9 hundredths _____ **5.** 56 hundredths _____

**6.** $\frac{84}{100}$ _____ **7.** $\frac{3}{10}$ _____ **8.** $\frac{1}{100}$ _____

**9.** 3 cents _____ **10.** 2 quarters _____ **11.** 3 nickels _____

Answer the questions below.

**12.** If you took a test with 10 questions and got 7 of them right, what decimal part would that be? _____ What decimal part did you get wrong? _____

**13.** If you had a dollar and spent 5 cents, what decimal amount did you spend? _____ What decimal amount do you have left? _____

**14.** If you had a bag of 100 beads and used 40, what decimal number did you use? Express this number in both tenths and hundredths. _____ _____

**15.** If you had to travel 100 miles and went 25, what decimal part of the trip did you travel? _____ What decimal part of the trip do you still have left? _____

# Remembering

**Name the fraction for each chain of fraction units.**

1. $\frac{1}{3} + \frac{1}{3}$ _____

2. $\frac{1}{6} + \frac{1}{6} + \frac{1}{6}$ _____

3. $\frac{1}{4} + \frac{1}{4} + \frac{1}{4}$ _____

4. $\frac{1}{12} + \frac{1}{12} + \frac{1}{12} + \frac{1}{12}$ _____

5. $\frac{1}{8} + \frac{1}{8} + \frac{1}{8} + \frac{1}{8} + \frac{1}{8}$ _____

6. $\frac{1}{8} + \frac{1}{8} + \frac{1}{8} + \frac{1}{8}$ _____

**Divide.**

7. $7\overline{)16}$    $7\overline{)32}$    $7\overline{)29}$    $7\overline{)86}$    $7\overline{)73}$    $7\overline{)90}$

8. $7\overline{)129}$    $7\overline{)108}$    $7\overline{)401}$    $7\overline{)304}$    $7\overline{)403}$    $7\overline{)158}$

**Solve.**

9. Kari made a cake shaped like a rectangle. She cut
the cake into 8 equal pieces. She and her mother each
ate one piece. What fraction of the cake was left? _____

**How many cubes were used to make each stack?**

10.

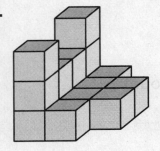

_____

11.

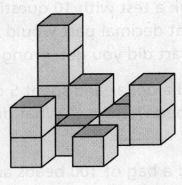

_____

12.

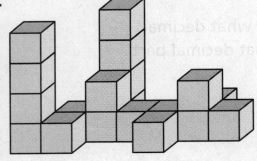

_____

Explore Decimal Numbers

**Name** _____ **Date** _____

# Homework

**Write the decimal numbers that come next.**

**1.** 0.05    0.06    0.07    _____    _____    _____    _____

**2.** 0.26    0.27    0.28    _____    _____    _____    _____

**3.** 0.3    0.4    0.5    _____    _____    _____    _____

**Write each number in decimal form.**

**4.** 9 tenths _____    **5.** 5 hundredths _____    **6.** 29 hundredths _____

**7.** $\frac{73}{100}$ _____    **8.** $\frac{2}{10}$ _____    **9.** $\frac{8}{100}$ _____

**10.** 4 pennies _____    **11.** 3 quarters _____    **12.** 6 dimes and 1 nickel _____

**Solve.**

A small jar contains 4 white gumballs and 6 red gumballs.

**13.** What decimal number shows which part of the gumballs are red? _____

**14.** What decimal number shows which part of the gumballs are white? _____

**15.** A large jar of 100 gumballs has the same fractions of red and white gumballs as the small jar. How many gumballs in the large jar are red? _____ How many are white? _____

A sidewalk has 100 squares. There are cracks in 9 of the squares.

**16.** What decimal number shows what part of the sidewalk is cracked? _____

**17.** What fraction shows what part of the sidewalk is cracked? _____

**Write each decimal tenth as a decimal hundredth.**

**18.** 0.6 = _____    **19.** 0.2 = _____    **20.** 0.5 = _____

# Remembering

**Complete each equation.**

1. $\frac{1}{4} +$ _____ $= \frac{4}{4} = 1$

2. _____ $+ \frac{5}{8} = \frac{8}{8} = 1$

3. $\frac{3}{6} +$ _____ $= \frac{6}{6} = 1$

4. _____ $+ \frac{2}{12} = \frac{12}{12} = 1$

5. $\frac{2}{7} +$ _____ $= \frac{7}{7} = 1$

6. _____ $+ \frac{4}{9} = \frac{9}{9} = 1$

7. $\frac{1}{3} +$ _____ $= \frac{3}{3} = 1$

8. _____ $+ \frac{1}{2} = \frac{2}{2} = 1$

**Divide.**

9. $8\overline{)21}$   10. $8\overline{)18}$   11. $8\overline{)97}$   12. $8\overline{)139}$

13. $8\overline{)142}$   14. $8\overline{)204}$   15. $8\overline{)135}$   16. $8\overline{)302}$

**Solve.**

17. In the school library, $\frac{6}{8}$ of the tables were filled with students. What fraction of the tables were not filled?

_____

**Tell whether each triangle is scalene, equilateral, or isosceles. Then tell whether each triangle is acute, right, or obtuse. Finally, find its perimeter.**

18.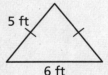
5 ft
6 ft

19.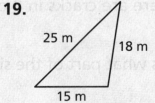
25 m
18 m
15 m

20.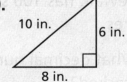
10 in.
6 in.
8 in.

Name: _____

Perimeter: _____

Name: _____

Perimeter: _____

Name: _____

Perimeter: _____

# Homework

**Write each number in decimal form.**

**1.** 6 tenths _____    **2.** 85 thousandths _____    **3.** 9 hundredths _____

**4.** 7 thousandths _____    **5.** $\frac{4}{100}$ _____    **6.** $2\frac{9}{10}$ _____

**7.** $\frac{915}{1,000}$ _____    **8.** $11\frac{3}{100}$ _____    **9.** 6 cents _____

**10.** twelve *and* 5 hundredths _____

**11.** thirty *and* 25 thousandths _____

**Use the graph to answer questions 12–14.**

**12.** What decimal part of all the melons did Amy pick? _____

**13.** What decimal part of all the melons did Paco pick? _____

**14.** What decimal part of all the melons did Joey and Lisa pick together? _____

**Melons Picked**

| | |
|------|--------------|
| Amy | ◯ |
| Joey | ◯ ◯ |
| Lisa | ◯ ◯ ◯ |
| Paco | ◯ ◯ ◯ ◯ |

Key: ◯ = 1 melon

**Solve.**

**15.** A centipede has 100 legs. What decimal part is one leg? _____

**16.** A millipede has 1,000 legs. What decimal part is 1 leg? _____

**17.** At a banquet, each cake was cut into 100 pieces. The guests ate 4 whole cakes and all but one piece of another. What decimal number represents the number of cakes that were eaten? _____

**18.** Miguel earned $10 and saved $3. What decimal part did he save? _____

**19.** Jing earned $100, and saved $30. What decimal part did she save? _____

**20.** Darnell earned $1,000, and saved $300. What decimal part did he save? _____

# Remembering

**Insert > or < to make a true statement.**

1. $\frac{2}{4}$ ◯ $\frac{2}{3}$

2. $\frac{3}{12}$ ◯ $\frac{4}{12}$

3. $\frac{3}{4}$ ◯ $\frac{3}{5}$

4. $\frac{2}{6}$ ◯ $\frac{2}{7}$

5. $\frac{7}{9}$ ◯ $\frac{7}{10}$

6. $\frac{1}{4}$ ◯ $\frac{2}{4}$

7. $\frac{5}{8}$ ◯ $\frac{4}{8}$

8. $\frac{10}{11}$ ◯ $\frac{10}{12}$

9. $\frac{2}{6}$ ◯ $\frac{3}{6}$

**Solve.**

*Show your work.*

10. Meg served $\frac{3}{7}$ of an apple pie and $\frac{1}{8}$ of a cherry pie of the same size. Which pie did she serve more of? Explain your thinking.

_____

_____

11. Kyle and Shawn each had the same size sandwich. Kyle ate $\frac{1}{3}$ of his sandwich. Shawn ate $\frac{1}{6}$ of his sandwich. Who ate more? Explain.

_____

_____

**Find the surface area of each prism. Explain how you got your answer.**

12.

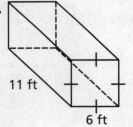

11 ft
6 ft

13.

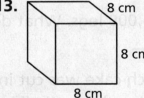

8 cm
8 cm
8 cm

_____     _____

_____     _____

_____     _____

_____     _____

**Name** _____ **Date** _____

# Homework

**Write these amounts as decimal numbers.**

**1.** 4 tenths _____

**2.** 72 thousandths _____

**3.** 9 hundredths _____

**4.** 8 cents _____

**5.** $\frac{68}{100}$ _____

**6.** $9\frac{4}{10}$ _____

**7.** $\frac{16}{1000}$ _____

**8.** $6\frac{7}{100}$ _____

**9.** 3 thousandths _____

**Circle the number that does not have the same value as the others.**

**10.** 0.95   0.950   0.905   0.95

**11.** 0.2   0.20   $\frac{2}{10}$   0.02

**12.** 0.730   0.703   0.73   0.73

**13.** 1.6   1.60   1.06   1.6000

**14.** 0.59   5.90   0.590   $\frac{59}{100}$

**15.** 0.08   0.008   0.08   0.080

**Insert < or > to make a true statement.**

**16.** 0.67 ◯ 0.7

**17.** 0.315 ◯ 0.42

**18.** 0.58 ◯ 0.5

**19.** 8.3 ◯ 0.83

**20.** 0.921 ◯ 0.912

**21.** 2.3 ◯ 0.84

**22.** 0.1 ◯ 0.01

**23.** 0.74 ◯ 0.714

**The table shows how far four students jumped in the long jump contest. Use the table to answer the questions.**

**24.** Whose jump was longest? _____

**25.** Whose jump was shortest? _____

**26.** Which two students jumped the same distance? _____

**Long Jump Contest**

| Name | Length of Jump |
|------|----------------|
| Joshua | 1.610 meters |
| Amanda | 1.592 meters |
| Hester | 1.7 meters |
| Miguel | 1.61 meters |

# Remembering

**Add or subtract.**

1. $\frac{2}{6} + \frac{3}{6} =$

2. $\frac{8}{9} - \frac{4}{9} =$

3. $\frac{7}{8} - \frac{5}{8} =$

4. $\frac{4}{7} + \frac{1}{7} =$

5. $\frac{9}{10} - \frac{3}{10} =$

6. $\frac{10}{12} - \frac{6}{12} =$

7. $\frac{2}{5} + \frac{2}{5} =$

8. $\frac{3}{4} - \frac{2}{4} =$

9. $\frac{6}{11} - \frac{4}{11} =$

**Solve.**

10. Lori ate $\frac{1}{4}$ of her sandwich at lunch. She ate $\frac{2}{4}$ more sandwich for a snack later on. How much of her sandwich is left?

_____

11. Felix cut a mushroom pizza into eighths. Jenny ate $\frac{2}{8}$ of the pizza. Felix ate $\frac{3}{8}$ of the pizza. What fraction of the pizza was left?

_____

12. Ben used a $\frac{1}{3}$-foot piece of string for an art project. Then he decided to use another $\frac{1}{3}$-foot piece of string. What was the total length of the strings Ben used?

_____

13. Missy made some cupcakes. She gave $\frac{4}{9}$ of the cupcakes to her sisters. She gave $\frac{1}{9}$ of the cupcakes to her brother. What fraction of the cupcakes did she have left?

_____

**Name each figure. Then tell the name of the shapes of its bases and faces.**

14.

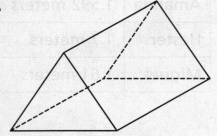

_____

_____

_____

15.

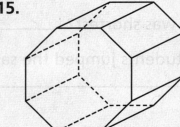

_____

_____

_____

       Compare Decimal Numbers

**Name** _____ **Date** _____

# Homework

**The number line below shows one whole divided into hundredths.**

**1.** What decimal hundredth is marked by the fish? _____

Round this number to the nearest tenth. _____

**2.** What decimal hundredth is marked by the dog? _____

Round this number to the nearest tenth. _____

**3.** What decimal hundredth is marked by the cat? _____

Round this number to the nearest tenth. _____

**4.** On the number line, draw arrows to mark 78 hundredths and to mark 9 tenths.

**Round to the nearest tenth.**

**5.** 0.31 _____

**6.** 0.93 _____

**7.** 0.57 _____

**8.** 0.25 _____

**9.** 1.19 _____

**10.** 5.08 _____

**Round to the nearest whole number.**

**11.** 6.7 _____

**12.** 5.3 _____

**13.** 14.5 _____

**14.** 29.7 _____

**15.** 8.39 _____

**16.** 3.07 _____

**17.** What is $13.92 rounded to the nearest dollar? _____

**18.** What is $0.43 rounded to the nearest tenth of a dollar, or dime? _____

**Name** _____ **Date** _____

# Remembering

**Solve the problems.**

*Show your work.*

1. Mrs. Kim ordered 2 sub sandwiches. One was 12 inches long. The other was 16 inches long. She cut each into 4 equal pieces. Which sub had larger pieces? Explain.

_____

_____

_____

2. Mike took 24 cookies to the picnic. Alma took 12 cookies to the picnic. At the end of the picnic, Mike had $\frac{1}{4}$ of his cookies left and Alma had $\frac{1}{3}$ of her cookies left. Who had more cookies left? Explain.

_____

_____

3. The math club has 14 members. The reading club has 18 members. Each club sent $\frac{1}{2}$ of its members to the monthly school meeting. Which club sent fewer members to the meeting? Explain.

_____

_____

4. Mr. Kane served $\frac{5}{8}$ of an apple pie and $\frac{5}{8}$ of a berry pie. The berry pie was larger than the apple pie. Which pie had a greater amount left? Explain.

_____

_____

_____

Number Lines and Rounding

## Homework

**On the number line below, estimate the positions of the following numbers. Plot and label a point for each number.**

**1.** $\frac{11}{12}$      **2.** $\frac{1}{4}$      **3.** $\frac{3}{5}$      **4.** 0.42      **5.** 0.76

**On the number line below, estimate the positions of the following numbers. Plot and label a point for each number.**

**6.** 3.09      **7.** 3.8      **8.** $3\frac{4}{9}$      **9.** $3\frac{5}{6}$      **10.** $3\frac{1}{2}$

**On the number line below, estimate the positions of the following numbers. Plot and label a point for each number.**

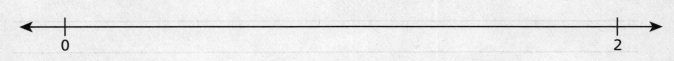

**11.** 1.94      **12.** 0.9      **13.** $1\frac{3}{4}$      **14.** $\frac{7}{10}$      **15.** $1\frac{1}{9}$

**Solve.**

**16.** Tamika estimated the point on the number line is $1\frac{7}{12}$. Do you agree or disagree? Explain your choice.

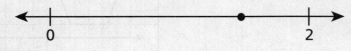

_____

_____

**Multiply.**

1. $34 \times 3 =$ _____

2. $629 \times 3 =$ _____

3. $67 \times 55 =$ _____

**Divide.**

4. $3\overline{)88}$

5. $9\overline{)389}$

6. $4\overline{)3,795}$

**Solve for *a*.**

7. $a + 210 = 415$
   $a =$ _____

8. $a - 210 = 415$
   $a =$ _____

9. $4a = 76$
   $a =$ _____

10. $a \div 4 = 76$
    $a =$ _____

**Solve.**

11. Kaitlyn and Jeremy found the prime factorization of 100. Kaitlyn wrote 4 • 5 • 5. Jeremy wrote 2 • 2 • 25. Are the prime factorizations correct? If not, correct them.

    _____

    _____

12. The school play starts at 6:30 P.M. The teacher wants everyone to the school 45 minutes before the play starts. It takes Jeremy 15 minutes to get to school. What time should he leave to get to school? _____

13. Explain the transformations that happened to the trapezoid.

    _____

    _____

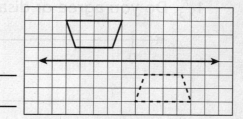

**Name** _____ **Date** _____

# Homework

**Solve.**

1. Look at the centimeter ruler below. Round the length of the string to the nearest centimeter. _____

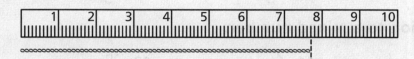

The table to the right shows the rainfall in 3 towns last month.

2. Which town had the most rain?

_____

3. Which town had the least rain?

_____

| Rainfall in Inches | |
|---|---|
| Beanville | 0.6 |
| Cloverdale | 0.131 |
| Wheatburg | 0.82 |

**Follow the directions for each number. Start with the original number each time.**

| 4.528 | 65.703 |
|---|---|

4. Make the number a tenth more.

_____

5. Make the number 0.01 less.

_____

6. Increase the digit in the ones place by 1.

_____

7. Decrease the digit in the thousandths place by 1.

_____

8. Make the number 10 more.

_____

9. Make the number 0.1 less.

_____

10. Increase the digit in the hundredths place by 1.

_____

11. Decrease the digit in the thousandths place by 1.

_____

# Remembering

**Change each mixed number to an improper fraction.**

1. $2\frac{3}{6}$ _____

2. $1\frac{9}{10}$ _____

3. $7\frac{8}{9}$ _____

4. $4\frac{5}{7}$ _____

5. $6\frac{2}{4}$ _____

6. $8\frac{4}{5}$ _____

7. $3\frac{6}{8}$ _____

8. $9\frac{1}{3}$ _____

**Change each improper fraction to a mixed number.**

9. $\frac{15}{2}$ _____

10. $\frac{38}{5}$ _____

11. $\frac{27}{4}$ _____

12. $\frac{36}{8}$ _____

13. $\frac{14}{3}$ _____

14. $\frac{55}{6}$ _____

15. $\frac{47}{9}$ _____

16. $\frac{65}{7}$ _____

**Solve.**

17. There were $4\frac{5}{8}$ pies in the case at the diner. Then 30 people each had $\frac{1}{8}$ of a pie. What fraction of a pie was left?

_____

18. Each person in a family of 8 people had $\frac{2}{6}$ of a sub. What mixed number tells how many subs the family ate in all?

_____

**Name the pyramid that would be made from the net when it is folded. Then name the shapes of the base and the faces.**

19.

_____

_____

_____

20.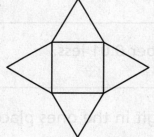

_____

_____

_____

Practice With Decimal Numbers

# Homework

**Add. Watch the place values.**

**1.** $37 + 21¢ = _____   **2.** 0.4 + 0.05 = _____   **3.** 73 + 0.32 = _____

**4.** $52.07 + 83¢ = _____   **5.** 0.56 + 0.19 = _____   **6.** 97.2 + 0.361 = _____

**7.** 18¢ + $6.29 = _____   **8.** 0.003 + 0.06 = _____   **9.** 83.27 + 4.5 = _____

**10.** Which sum is incorrect? Explain why.

    **A.** 45 + 0.38 = 45.38      **B.** 67¢ + $54 = $54.67      **C.** 0.14 + 0.5 = 0.19

_____

_____

_____

**Solve.**                                                                     *Show your work.*

**11.** Yesterday, the snow was 4.68 centimeters deep. Last
night 0.3 centimeters of new snow fell. How deep
is the snow now?

_____

**12.** Dana walks 0.4 miles to the bus stop and then rides
the bus 3.05 miles to school. How far away is Dana's
school?

_____

**13.** Cowboy Jones is 1.95 meters tall. His cowboy hat
makes him 0.09 meters taller. How tall is Cowboy
Jones when he is wearing his hat?

_____

# Remembering

**Follow the directions for each number. Start with the original number each time.**

1.623

**1.** Make the number a tenth more. _____

**2.** Make the number 0.01 less. _____

**3.** Increase the digit in the ones place by 1. _____

**4.** Decrease the digit in the thousandths place by 1. _____

4.075

**5.** Make the number 2 tenths more. _____

**6.** Make the number 0.001 less. _____

**7.** Increase the digit in the ones place by 3. _____

**8.** Decrease the digit in the hundredths place by 1. _____

**Add or subtract.**

**9.** $\frac{3}{2} + \frac{1}{2} =$

**10.** $\frac{12}{8} - \frac{7}{8} =$

**11.** $\frac{11}{9} - \frac{5}{9} =$

**12.** $3\frac{2}{4}$
$+ 5\frac{3}{4}$

**13.** $8\frac{9}{10}$
$+ 4\frac{5}{10}$

**14.** $9\frac{4}{7}$
$+ 2\frac{6}{7}$

**15.** $6\frac{2}{3}$
$+ 7\frac{2}{3}$

**16.** $4\frac{4}{5}$
$- 1\frac{2}{5}$

**17.** $9\frac{3}{8}$
$- 4\frac{6}{8}$

**18.** $8\frac{7}{9}$
$- 6\frac{5}{9}$

**19.** $6\frac{1}{6}$
$- 5\frac{4}{6}$

**Solve.**

**20.** Annie had 2 oranges. She cut each orange into sixths. She used 8 sixths to make a fruit salad. What fraction of an orange was left?

_____

**21.** Some friends bought 3 pizzas. Each pizza was cut into eighths. The friends ate 18 slices. What fraction of a pizza was left?

_____

Add Decimal Numbers

**Name** _____ **Date** _____

# Homework

**Find the difference. Use a separate sheet of paper if necessary.**

**1.** $59 − 14¢ = _____

**2.** 0.4 − 0.07 = _____

**3.** 26 − 0.36 = _____

**4.** $42.06 − 23¢ = _____

**5.** 0.95 − 0.38 = _____

**6.** 67 − 0.49 = _____

**7.** 0.87 − 0.19 = _____

**8.** 0.16 − 0.004 = _____

**9.** 52.17 − 1.09 = _____

**Solve.**

*Show your work.*

**10.** A scientist found two dinosaur tracks. One was 70.36 centimeters long, and the other was 91.405 centimeters long. What is the difference in the sizes of the tracks?

_____

**11.** A race is 5.65 kilometers long. Paolo has run 3.48 kilometers so far. How much farther does he need to run?

_____

**12.** A caterpillar was 0.452 centimeters long when it hatched. Since then, it has grown 0.5 centimeters. How long is the caterpillar now?

_____

**13.** A recipe calls for 0.85 pounds of dark chocolate and 0.7 pounds of white chocolate. How much chocolate is needed altogether?

_____

**14.** Carla's pet rat weighs 0.905 pounds, and Jenny's weighs 0.78 pounds. Which rat is smaller? How much smaller?

_____

# Remembering

**Add or subtract.**

1. $\frac{10}{11} - \frac{2}{3} =$

2. $\frac{9}{6} + \frac{7}{3} =$

3. $1\frac{3}{8} - \frac{3}{5} =$

**Subtract the smaller number from the larger number.**

4. $1\frac{5}{6}; \frac{8}{6}$

5. $\frac{15}{9}; 2\frac{3}{9}$

6. $6\frac{7}{8}; 7\frac{5}{8}$

**Solve.**                                                   *Show your work.*

7. Karina is walking a trail that is $1\frac{1}{3}$ miles long. So far, she has walked $\frac{1}{6}$ of a mile. How far does she still have left to walk?

_____

_____

8. Terrell rode his bicycle $\frac{3}{5}$ of a mile to the store. Then he rode $\frac{2}{4}$ of a mile to school. How many miles did he ride in all?

_____

**Name the prism that has each shape as its bases.**

9.
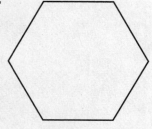

_____

10.
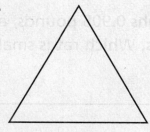

_____

Subtract Decimal Numbers

# Homework

**A $5 bill was used to buy each item below. List the coins and bills you would use to make change.**

**1.**

$2.29

_____

_____

**2.**

$4.37

_____

_____

**A $10 bill was used to buy each item below. List the coins and bills you would use to make change.**

**3.**

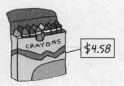

$4.58

_____

_____

**4.**

$1.96

_____

_____

**Write the names and numbers of coins and bills you would use to make change for each of the following.**

**5.** The cost of an item is $1.59. You give the clerk 1 one-dollar bill and 3 quarters.

_____

**6.** The cost of an item is 83¢. You give the clerk 9 dimes.

_____

**Solve.**

**7.** Paulos bought a cap for $11.61. He paid with 1 $10 bill and 1 $5 bill. Paulos receives 2 $1 bills, 5 quarters, 1 dime, and 4 pennies in change. Is this correct? If not, what is the correct change? If so, show a different way to give the change.

_____

**Name** _____ **Date** _____

# Remembering

**Multiply.**

**1.** $26 \times 5 =$ _____

**2.** $346 \times 2 =$ _____

**3.** $54 \times 39 =$ _____

**Divide.**

**4.** $74 \div 7 =$ _____

**5.** $325 \div 3 =$ _____

**6.** $5,589 \div 6 =$ _____

**Find a reasonable estimate for each problem.**

**7.** $69 \times 34$ _____

**8.** $71 \div 4$ _____

**Use mental math to find the value for *n*.**

**9.** $2n - 6 = 8$
 $n =$ _____

**10.** $2n + 6 = 8$
 $n =$ _____

**11.** $3n - 7 = 14$
 $n =$ _____

**12.** $3n + 8 = 14$
 $n =$ _____

**Solve.**

**13.** On Monday, Daniel bought items at three stores. He spent $5.11 at the bookstore, $28.16 at the grocery store, and $20.01 at the music store. He had $2.29 left when he was done shopping at the three stores. How much money did he have before he started shopping? _____

**14.** Look at Figure A. Circle the shaded figure that shows how Figure A looks after it is rotated 180° clockwise.

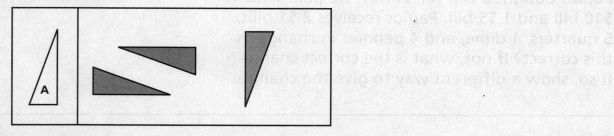

Making Change

# Homework

**Estimate the answers by rounding to the nearest tenth.**

**1.** 0.49 − 0.17   About _____   **2.** 0.91 − 0.07   About _____

**3.** 0.32 + 0.21   About _____   **4.** 0.65 − 0.38   About _____

**5.** 0.87 − 0.34   About _____   **6.** 0.18 + 0.04   About _____

**Estimate the answers by rounding to the nearest whole number.**

**7.** 3.49 + 5.17   About _____   **8.** 8.91 − 0.97   About _____

**9.** 9.32 − 3.81   About _____   **10.** 5.65 + 1.98   About _____

**11.** 11.87 + 1.39   About _____   **12.** 24.18 − 3.14   About _____

**Use estimation to answer the following questions.**

**13.** Ernesto wants to buy a sleeping bag for $79.89 and a flashlight for $9.16. He has $89.00. Does he have enough money? Explain.

_____

_____

_____

**14.** Mr. Reyes has $2.50 in his pocket. He wants to buy a toothbrush for $0.95 and a bar of soap for $1.49. Does he have enough money? Explain.

_____

_____

_____

**Estimate each answer by rounding to the nearest tenth. Then find the exact answer.**

**15.** 0.656 − 0.37   Estimated Answer _____   Exact Answer _____

**16.** 0.09 + 0.801   Estimated Answer _____   Exact Answer _____

**17.** 0.79 − 0.310   Estimated Answer _____   Exact Answer _____

# Remembering

**Divide.**

**1.** 5)196      **2.** 3)83      **3.** 4)91

**4.** 6)75      **5.** 7)95      **6.** 9)88

**7.** 4)313      **8.** 8)975      **9.** 2)517

**10.** 3)265      **11.** 6)164      **12.** 5)359

**13.** 8)2,198      **14.** 7)1,713      **15.** 9)3,212

**Solve.**

**16.** Milton packs milk bottles into crates. Each crate has 4 rows and can fit 7 bottles in each row. If Milton has 224 bottles, how many rows can he fill?

_____

**17.** Selena wants to make 8 necklaces with the same number of beads in each necklace. If she has 584 beads, what is the greatest number of beads she can use for each necklace?

_____

**Find the perimeter and area of each triangle.**

**18.**

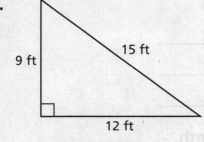

9 ft   15 ft   12 ft

Perimeter: _____

Area: _____

**19.**

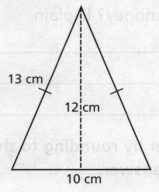

13 cm   12 cm   10 cm

Perimeter: _____

Area: _____

Estimate With Decimal Numbers

The Scaly Creatures Reptile Park has animals such as turtles, snakes, alligators, and crocodiles. Answer the questions about the reptiles.

**1.** Last year, the largest alligator, Alex, was 3.9 meters long. This year Alex is 4.15 meters long. How much did Alex grow in one year?

_____

**2.** The turtles are fed 12.75 pounds of food in the morning and 10.5 pounds in the evening. How much food do they get each day?

_____

**3.** Giant tortoises can grow to be 1.4 meters long. Shelley the tortoise is 0.65 meters long. How much longer could she get?

_____

**4.** Crocodiles can live to be 75 years old. The oldest crocodile in the park, Olga, is now 63.5 years old. How much longer could she live?

_____

**5.** One of the rattlesnakes was 5.85 centimeters long when she hatched last year. During the year, she grew 7.65 centimeters. How long is she now?

_____

**6.** The largest python at the park weighs 31.72 pounds. The smallest python weighs 9.08 pounds. What is the difference in their weights?

_____

**Subtract.**

**7.** $46 − 19¢ = _____

**8.** 0.5 − 0.07 = _____

**9.** 36 − 0.16 = _____

**10.** $52.09 − 36¢ = _____

**11.** 0.85 − 0.58 = _____

**12.** 97.2 − 0.24 = _____

**13.** 0.67 − 0.19 = _____

**14.** 0.15 − 0.003 = _____

**15.** 42.18 − 1.07 = _____

## Divide. Write the quotient with a remainder.

**1.** 5)4,793

**2.** 3)2,351

**3.** 4)9,083

**4.** 7)6,204

**5.** 9)9,918

**6.** 6)8,795

## Divide.

**7.** 2)$56.18

**8.** 7)$90.02

**9.** 8)$25.36

## Find the perimeter and area of each figure.

**10.**

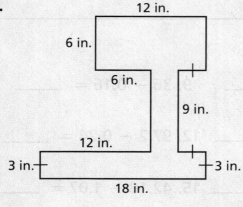

Perimeter: _____

Area: _____

**11.**

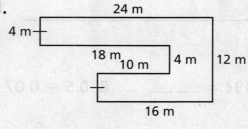

Perimeter: _____

Area: _____

Mixed Practice With Decimals

**Homework**

The list below shows the amount of fruit purchased from the market.

**Fruit Purchases (lb = pounds)**

| apples $4\frac{3}{7}$ lb | bananas $2\frac{3}{8}$ lb |
|---|---|
| grapes $3\frac{11}{12}$ lb | oranges $3\frac{1}{10}$ lb |

Decide if each weight is closer to a half pound or to a whole pound. Then *estimate* the total weight of these purchases.

**1.** grapes + bananas

_____

**2.** bananas + apples

_____

**3.** oranges + grapes

_____

**4.** apples + oranges

_____

The list below shows a variety of fabric and lengths.

**Fabric (yd = yards)**

| Denim  0.6 yd | Linen  1.9 yd |
|---|---|
| Cotton  1.3 yd | Silk  2.1 yd |

Decide if each length is closer to $\frac{1}{2}$ yard, $1\frac{1}{2}$ yards, or 2 yards. Then *estimate* the total yards in each fabric combination.

**5.** Denim + Cotton _____

**6.** Linen + Silk _____

**7.** Cotton + Linen _____

**8.** Denim + Linen _____

**Solve.**

**9.** Tony needs about 5 yards of fabric to make a quilt. If he buys all four fabric pieces, does he have enough fabric to make the quilt? Explain your answer.

_____

_____

Estimate Using Benchmarks

# Remembering

**Multiply.**

**1.** 79 × 4 = _____   **2.** 871 × 5 = _____   **3.** 92 × 78 = _____

**Divide.**

**4.** 90 ÷ 6 = _____   **5.** 486 ÷ 5 = _____   **6.** 4,036 ÷ 3 = _____

**Simplify each expression.**

**7.** 24 − 6 • 2 = _____   **8.** 7 + 3 • (2 + 5) = _____   **9.** (9c + 4c) − 7c = _____

**Solve.**

**10.** Ms. Scott bought 3 packages with 24 pens
in each package. After she gave each of
her students three pens, she had 12 pens left.
How many students does Ms. Scott have?

_____

**11.** Monica left school at 4:45 P.M. She had basketball
practice for 1 hour and 15 minutes and classes for
7 hours. At what time did school start?

_____

**Use a protractor to measure each angle.**

**12.**

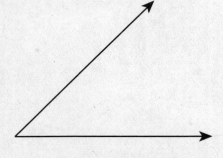

_____

**13.**

_____

Estimate Using Benchmarks

# Homework

## 1. Connections

At a track meet, four people jumped in a high jump event. Jason jumped 1.02 meters. Eric jumped 0.98 meters. Pedro jumped 1.24 meters. Ken jumped 1.2 meters. Order the contestants from highest jump to lowest.

_____

## 2. Reasoning and Proof

Mori is thinking of a number with two decimal places that is less than 1. The digit in the tenths place is an odd number. The digit in the hundredths place is 7 less than the digit in the tenths place. What number is Mori thinking of? Explain your reasoning.

_____

## 3. Communication

Bill says that only some zeros in decimal number are important. Is Bill correct? Explain why or why not.

_____

_____

_____

## 4. Representation

Susan rounded 0.9 to 0.10 on a math test. Did she round correctly? Use pictures to help explain your answer.

_____

_____

**Name** _____ **Date** _____

# Remembering

**Divide. Write the quotient with a remainder.**

1. 5)3,843

2. 4)4,502

3. 3)1,795

4. 7)7,377

5. 6)1,788

6. 5)3,823

**Solve.**

7. Jason has 252 boxes. He wants to place 6 books in each box. How many boxes will he fill?

_____

8. Lupe has 220 photos from her vacation. She wants to place them in a photo album and can put 9 photos on a page. How many pages will she fill?

_____

**Find the perimeter and area of each figure.**

9.

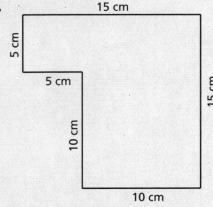

Perimeter: _____

Area: _____

10.

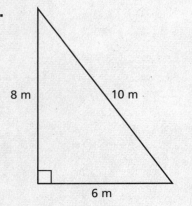

Perimeter: _____

Area: _____

Use Mathematical Processes

**Name** _____ **Date** _____

# Homework

**Write the measurement marked on each ruler.**

**1.**
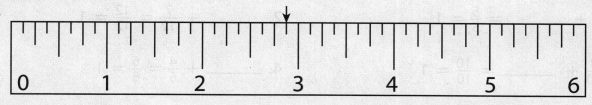

**2.**

**3.**
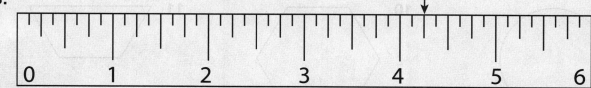

**Measure each line segment to the nearest $\frac{1}{8}$ inch.**

**4.** •————————————————•

_____

**5.** •—————————————————————————•

_____

**6.** •——————————————————•

_____

**7.** •—————————————————————————————•

_____

**Draw a line segment with the length shown.**

**8.** $4\frac{7}{8}$ inches

**9.** $2\frac{3}{8}$ inches

**10.** $3\frac{1}{2}$ inches

# Remembering

**Complete each equation.**

1. $\frac{2}{5} +$ _____ $= \frac{5}{5} = 1$

2. _____ $+ \frac{7}{12} = \frac{12}{12} = 1$

3. $\frac{8}{10} +$ _____ $= \frac{10}{10} = 1$

4. _____ $+ \frac{4}{6} = \frac{6}{6} = 1$

5. $\frac{5}{9} +$ _____ $= \frac{9}{9} = 1$

6. _____ $+ \frac{3}{4} = \frac{4}{4} = 1$

7. $\frac{6}{7} +$ _____ $= \frac{7}{7} = 1$

8. _____ $+ \frac{1}{8} = \frac{8}{8} = 1$

**Name each plane figure.**

9.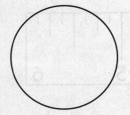

_____

10.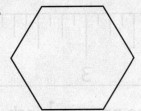

_____

11.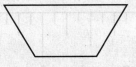

_____

**Name each solid.**

12.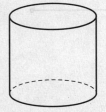

_____

13.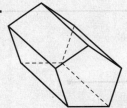

_____

14.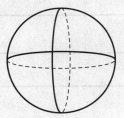

_____

**Solve.**

15. Amanda checked out 7 books with 64 pages each. She also checked out 4 books with 89 pages each. How many total pages is Amanda going to read?

_____

Length

**Name** _____ **Date** _____

# Homework

**Solve.**                                                                 *Show your work.*

1. Denzel's father installed carpet tiles in the family room. The room is 12 feet by 16 feet. Each tile measured 1 square foot. How many tiles did he use?

   _____

2. Brady built a doghouse for his new puppy. The inside of the doghouse measured 2 feet wide, 3 feet deep, and 4 feet tall. How many cubic feet of space are inside the doghouse?

   _____

3. A play area measures 20 yards long and 15 yards wide. It costs $2.00 per square yard to cover the area with wood chips. What is the cost of new wood chips for the entire play area?

   _____

4. Awan keeps his art supplies in a special box. The box is 18 inches long, 9 inches wide, and 6 inches deep. How many cubic inches of space are inside the box?

   _____

**Solve each problem about objects in your home.**

5. Measure the area of an object at home. Name the object and the unit or units you used to measure its area.

   _____

   _____

6. Measure the volume of an object at home. Name the object and the unit or units you used to measure its volume.

   _____

   _____

**Name** _____ **Date** _____

# Remembering

**Write a > or < to compare the fractions.**

1. $\frac{3}{6}$ ____ $\frac{3}{5}$

2. $\frac{6}{10}$ ____ $\frac{7}{10}$

3. $\frac{2}{3}$ ____ $\frac{2}{4}$

4. $\frac{4}{7}$ ____ $\frac{3}{7}$

5. $\frac{3}{9}$ ____ $\frac{3}{8}$

6. $\frac{10}{15}$ ____ $\frac{9}{15}$

**Add or subtract.**

7. $\frac{2}{9} + \frac{5}{9} =$ _____

8. $\frac{2}{5} + 3\frac{1}{5} =$ _____

9. $1\frac{4}{10} - \frac{9}{10} =$ _____

10. $2\frac{3}{4} + \frac{3}{8} =$ _____

11. $\frac{3}{2} + \frac{2}{5} =$ _____

12. $5\frac{1}{6} - 1\frac{2}{3} =$ _____

**How many cubes can you see in each stack?**
**How many cubes can you not see?**
**How many cubes total are in each stack?**

13.

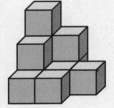

____ cubes can be
seen

____ cubes cannot be
seen

____ cubes total

14.

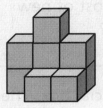

____ cubes can be
seen

____ cube cannot be
seen

____ cubes total

15.

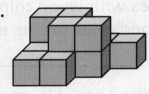

____ cubes can be
seen

____ cubes cannot be
seen

____ cubes total

16. Inez bought 3 pairs of socks for $2.35 each and a hat for
$6.95. She paid with a $20 bill. How much change should
she receive?

_____

17. Ali received $5.65 change from a $20 bill. He bought a
present for $11.95 and a card. What was the cost of
the card?

_____

Square and Cubic Measurement

**Solve. Remember: 1 pound = 16 ounces.**  *Show your work.*

1. A female rabbit gave birth to 6 babies. Each baby weighed 4 ounces. How many ounces did the babies weigh in all?

   _____

2. One watermelon weighs 8 pounds 2 ounces. Another weighs 7 pounds 12 ounces. Which watermelon is heavier? By how many ounces?

   _____

3. A box of cereal weighs 21 ounces. Does it weigh more or less than 1 pound? How much more or less?

   _____

4. At the beginning of the school year, Jared's dog weighed $46\frac{1}{2}$ pounds. At the end of the school year, it weighed 50 pounds. How much weight did Jared's dog gain during that time? How many ounces is this?

   _____

5. Claire has 8 books. Each book weighs 8 ounces. How many pounds do her books weigh altogether?

   _____

6. A bread recipe calls for $6\frac{1}{4}$ pounds of flour. How many batches of bread can a baker make with 25 pounds of flour?

   _____

# Remembering

**Solve on a separate sheet of paper.**

**1.** 5)93          **2.** 9)513          **3.** 7)764          **4.** 8)7,235

**5.** 4)54          **6.** 6)624          **7.** 4)861          **8.** 6)9,387

**9.** 7)75          **10.** 2)734          **11.** 3)970          **12.** 2)5,678

**13.** 3)66          **14.** 8)538          **15.** 5)477          **16.** 9)7,805

**17.** Check two of your divisions by multiplying and adding the remainder.

_____

**Is each figure a net for a cube? Write yes or no.**

**18.** 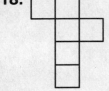          **19.**           **20.**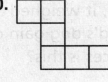

_____          _____          _____

**Solve.**                                                    *Show your work.*

**21.** There are 6 pennies, 5 dimes, and 4 quarters in Josela's pocket. What fraction of the coins are pennies?

_____

**22.** Luis and Sasha have identical notebooks. Luis's notebook is $\frac{3}{4}$ full. Sasha's notebook is $\frac{5}{8}$ full. Whose notebook has less space remaining?

_____

Weight

# Homework

Percy and Grace are making a birthday cake for their father. Their only measuring container holds $\frac{1}{4}$ cup.

**Solve.**

*Show your work.*

1. They need 2 cups of flour. How many $\frac{1}{4}$ cups should they measure?

   _____

2. They need $1\frac{1}{2}$ cups of sugar. How many $\frac{1}{4}$ cups should they measure?

   _____

3. The recipe calls for $\frac{3}{4}$ cup of cocoa. How many $\frac{1}{4}$ cups of cocoa should they measure?

   _____

4. The recipe calls for $\frac{1}{8}$ cup of oil. How can they use their $\frac{1}{4}$ cup to measure the oil they need?

   _____

5. Write and solve your own measurement word problem that uses fractions.

   _____

   _____

   _____

   _____

   _____

   _____

**Name** _____  **Date** _____

# Remembering

**Solve on a separate sheet of paper.**

1. 37,619 + 24,850

2. 867,027 − 9,436

3. 630,631 − 9,747

4. 2,604,925 + 3,687

5. 437,025 − 18,094

6. 320,705 − 56,923

7. 17,491 + 820,623

8. 7,586,742 − 87,604

9. 746,502 − 75,575

**Name each triangle by letters, angles, and sides.**

10.
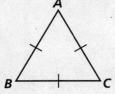

_____

_____

_____

11.
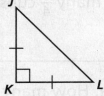

_____

_____

12.
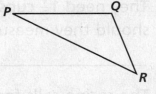

_____

_____

**Make a sketch to match the description.**

13. intersecting lines

14. parallel lines

15. perpendicular lines

**Solve.**

16. In how many different ways can Dwayne, Peter, and Marta stand in a line?

_____

17. Five teams are competing in a basketball tournament. Each team must play one game with every team in the tournament. How many games altogether will be played in the tournament?

_____

# Homework

**Solve.**

*Show your work.*

1. Sancho practices his trumpet every day from quarter to 5 to quarter past 5. How many minutes a day does he practice? How many hours?

   _____

2. Ella and her brother are going to a movie. It starts at quarter past 5 and lasts $2\frac{1}{4}$ hours. At what time will the movie end?

   _____

3. Jenn has soccer practice for $\frac{3}{4}$ of an hour on Tuesdays and Thursdays, and a game that lasts for about 1 hour on Saturdays. How many hours does she spend at soccer each week?

   _____

4. Before a storm, the outside temperature was 65°F. The storm caused the temperature to drop by 21°F. What was the outside temperature after the storm?

   _____

5. Write and solve your own word problem about time or temperature.

   _____

   _____

   _____

   _____

   _____

**Name** _____ **Date** _____

# Remembering

**Solve on a separate sheet of paper.**

1. $6 \times 80$      2. $3 \times 139$      3. $37 \times 18$      4. $7 \times 900$

5. $5 \times 228$      6. $25 \times 25$      7. $3 \times 4,000$      8. $31 \times 48$

9. $46 \times 85$      10. $7 \times 467$      11. $45 \times 14$      12. $45 \times 50$

**Find the surface area of each prism.**

13.

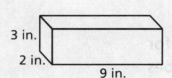

14.

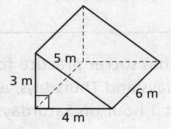

_____              _____

**Solve.**

15. In Lian's collection of 42 stamps, $\frac{2}{3}$ of the stamps are from foreign countries. In Mark's collection of 42 stamps, $\frac{3}{7}$ of the stamps are from foreign countries. Who has collected the greater number of foreign stamps?

_____

16. Laura is $\frac{1}{7}$ as old as her grandfather. If her grandfather is 63 years old, how much older is her grandfather than Laura?

_____

**Convert.**

17. 4 in. = _____ ft              18. 6 yd = _____ ft

19. 8 oz = _____ lb              20. 2,500 lb = _____ t

21. 3 c = _____ fl oz              22. 6 qt = _____ gal

Time and Temperature

**Name** _____ **Date** _____

# Homework

**Write the missing percent or the missing numerator or denominator.**

**1.** $65\% = \frac{65}{\phantom{0}} = \frac{\phantom{0}}{20}$

**2.** $80\% = \frac{\phantom{0}}{100} = \frac{4}{\phantom{0}}$

**3.** _____$\% = \frac{30}{100} = \frac{\phantom{0}}{10}$

**4.** _____$\% = \frac{35}{100} = \frac{7}{\phantom{0}}$

**5.** $\frac{2}{5} = \frac{\phantom{0}}{100} = $ _____$\%$

**6.** $\frac{11}{20} = \frac{\phantom{0}}{100} = $ _____$\%$

**Write the equivalent decimal or percent.**

**7.** $0.13 = $ _____$\%$

**8.** $0.05 = $ _____$\%$

**9.** $0.6 = $ _____$\%$

**10.** _____ $= 29\%$

**11.** _____ $= 6\%$

**12.** _____ $= 80\%$

**Complete each row in the table by writing the missing numerators or percents.**

| | Fraction | Percent | Decimal |
|---|---|---|---|
| **13.** | $\frac{44}{100} = \frac{\phantom{0}}{25}$ | 44% | _____ |
| **14.** | $\frac{\phantom{0}}{100}$ | 39% | _____ |
| **15.** | $\frac{1}{4} = \frac{\phantom{0}}{100}$ | 25% | _____ |

**Solve.**

**16.** Tara read 0.45 of her book. Marco read $\frac{3}{5}$ of his book. Calvin read 55% of his book. Each book has the same number of pages. Who has read the least number of pages? Explain how you found your answer.

_____

_____

**Explain how to change a whole number, a decimal number in tenths, and a decimal number in hundredths, to a percent. Include an example of each change in your explanation.**

_____

_____

_____

_____

_____

_____

_____

_____

_____

_____

_____

_____

_____

**Use the unit rate to complete each table.**

1.

| Unit Rate: $4 per pound | | | | | | | |
|---|---|---|---|---|---|---|---|
| **Pounds of Apples** | 1 | 2 | 3 | 4 | 5 | 6 | 7 |
| **Cost** | | | | | | | |

2.

| Unit Rate: 65 miles per hour (mph) | | | | | | | |
|---|---|---|---|---|---|---|---|
| **Time (in hours)** | 1 | 2 | 3 | 6 | 7 | 9 | 11 |
| **Distance (in miles)** | | | | | | | |

**Use the table in exercise 1 to help solve each problem.**

3. Shakira spent $36 on apples for her bakery. How many pounds of apples did she buy?

_____

4. Kyle has $55 to spend on 13 pounds of apples. Is this enough money to buy the apples? Explain.

_____

**Use the table in exercise 2 to help solve each problem.**

5. Antonio drove 260 miles at the given unit rate. For how many hours did he drive? _____

6. If George drives at a unit rate of 70 miles per hour, will he increase or decrease his average distance driven per hour? Give an example to support your answer.

_____

**Solve.**

7. The unit cost of one pencil is 17¢. What is the cost of twenty-three pencils? _____

8. A market sells 4 pounds of oranges for $12. What is the unit rate per pound for oranges? _____

9. A store sells a 7-ounce container of grape juice for $2.38 and a 15-ounce container for $4.80. Which container costs less per ounce? Explain.

_____

_____

# Homework

**Write a situation that includes a rate that is not a unit rate. Explain why a unit rate would be easier to understand.**

_____

_____

_____

_____

_____

_____

_____

_____

_____

_____

_____

_____

_____

_____

_____

_____

_____

_____

_____

Rates

**There are 24 students and 11 teachers on a bus. Use this information to write a ratio for each question.**

1. What is the ratio of teachers to students? _____

2. What is the ratio of teachers to the total number of people on the bus? _____

**Use the information in the exercises below to complete the ratio tables at the right. Then ask ratio questions of your classmates that can be answered using the tables.**

3. Wayne is writing a book. The book will have 35 pages in each chapter. Complete Table 3 to show the number of chapters (c) for multiples of 35 pages (p).

4. The class is starting a new sewing project that uses 8 inches of red fabric for every 9 inches of blue fabric. In the first row of Table 4, write the ratio of inches of blue fabric (b) to inches of red fabric (r). Then complete Table 4.

5. Jacob uses 3 cups of raisins for every 2 cups of cherries. In the first row of Table 5, write the ratio of cups of raisins (r) to cups of cherries (c). Then complete Table 5.

**Solve.**

6. Carmen has 15 cups of water and 9 cups of milk. She needs to mix water and milk in the ratio of 4 cups of water to 3 cups of milk. What is the greatest amount of each ingredient that she can use?

_____

**Table 3**

| (c) | (p) |
|-----|-----|
| 1   | 35  |
| 3   |     |
| 7   |     |
|     | 525 |
| 5   |     |
|     | 700 |

**Table 4**

| (b) | (r) |
|-----|-----|
| 45  |     |
|     | 24  |
|     | 80  |
| 135 |     |
| 99  |     |

**Table 5**

| (r) | (c) |
|-----|-----|
|     | 10  |
|     | 16  |
| 30  |     |
|     | 24  |
|     | 22  |

# Homework

**Write a situation that includes a ratio that is not
in simplest form. Explain why the simplest form of
the ratio would be easier to understand.**

_____

_____

_____

_____

_____

_____

_____

_____

_____

_____

_____

_____

_____

_____

_____

_____